Making Sense of Your New ESOP: A Leader's Guide

KENNETH E. SERWINSKI AND MICHAEL J. McGINLEY

Prairie Capital Advisors, Inc.
Oakbrook Terrace, Illinois

Copyright © 2019 by Prairie Capital Advisors, Inc.

All rights reserved. No part of this publication may be reproduced, distributed, or transmitted in any form or by any means, including photocopying or other electronic or mechanical methods, without prior written permission from the publisher.

The advice and strategies found within this book may not be suitable for every situation. This work is sold with the understanding that neither the authors nor the publisher are held responsible for the results that may transpire from acting upon the advice in this book.

ISBN: 978-1-7332613-1-9

Table of Contents

Introduction v

PART 1: WHAT SHOULD THE ESOP PARTICIPANTS KNOW?

Chapter 1   Rolling Out the ESOP to Participants 3

Chapter 2   ESOP Stock: Who Gets It? What Happens to It? And, How Do Participants Get Paid? 9

Chapter 3   The Rights of ESOP Participants 17

PART 2: WHO DOES WHAT?

Chapter 4   Board of Directors 23
Section 1 – Board of Directors Overview 23
Section 2 – The Evolution of the ESOP: Repurchase Obligation and Sustainability 31
Section 3 – ESOP Administration Committee 42
Section 4 – ESOP Plan Administrator 46

Chapter 5   The Management Team 51

Chapter 6   The ESOP Trustee 55
Section 1 – The ESOP Trustee Overview 55
Section 2 – ESOP Valuation 61
Section 3 – ESOP Legal Counsel 66

Chapter 7   ESOP Communications Committee 69

PART 3: WHAT ARE WE MISSING?

Chapter 8 Driving Value: How Personal Finance Literacy, Business Literacy, and Value Drivers Are Interrelated 75

Chapter 9 Preparing for the Possible Sale of the ESOP Company 87

PART 4: WHAT MIGHT OUR POST-CLOSING CHECKLIST INCLUDE? 96

Conclusion 107
Acknowledgements 109
Further Reading 111
References 113
About Prairie Capital Advisors, Inc. 117
About the Authors 118
Index 120

Introduction

You've become an **ESOP** company! Congratulations! Now what?

As a co-founder of Prairie Capital Advisors, I have had the opportunity to congratulate many ESOP companies on becoming employee-owned over the last 30 years. Over that period of time, immediately following the closing of an ESOP deal, I have heard and seen emotions that range from relief to outright joy! But I have also seen a little bit of fear as well…fear of what needs to happen next.

Oftentimes, CEOs of new ESOP companies tell me something to the effect of, "Sure seems like we had a lot of people working on our deal, but since we closed, I haven't seen anyone." Now, of course, that may be a bit of an exaggeration. You will have an annual valuation performed for the Trustee, and you will communicate the stock price to participants with their annual statements. You might even attend an ESOP conference sponsored by the National Center for Employee Ownership, The ESOP Association, or the Employee-Owned S Corporations of America. At the same time, you need to run the company well because you probably have some significant debt to repay.

Previously, under the watchful eye of founding shareholders, strategic and operational decisions were made to benefit one group…them. Now, the Board of Directors, perhaps with some new independent members, has appointed a CEO to enhance the value of the company for a new constituency – ESOP plan participants.

What's next? Well, we can't tell you how to run your business, but we do have a lot of knowledge and advice to share as leading professionals in the ESOP community. We have seen many successful ESOPs and learned from some of the smartest professionals in the ESOP community. Further, we have advised over 500 companies on various issues that arise in running an ESOP company. In addition, Prairie Capital Advisors itself is a fractional ESOP company with 11 non-ESOP shareholders, so we not only prescribe but also take our own medicine.

By providing this handbook, we hope to help guide you through the complex world of ESOPs. We map out best practices for the board, management, and advisors at 100% ESOP-owned S corporations. Toward the back of the book, we have also included a post-closing checklist of action items and tasks. We want ESOP companies to be the best they can be because we all understand the power of successful employee ownership.

Best of luck to you on your new adventure!

KENNETH E. SERWINSKI

Chairman

Prairie Capital Advisors, Inc.

June 2019

PART 1

What Should the ESOP Participants Know?

CHAPTER 1

Rolling Out the ESOP to Participants

NOW that you have completed the process of implementing an ESOP, the real fun can begin! Typically, once a company becomes employee-owned, the seller and the management team are very excited to be able to share this information with the company's employees.

Shortly after the ESOP is implemented, one of the first steps a company should take is to introduce the concept of the ESOP to its employees. The first communication to employees, typically made within the days or weeks after the ESOP is implemented, is usually a very brief initial announcement of the ESOP transaction along with an assurance that more details regarding the ESOP are to come. At this point, employees are often unaware that the ESOP transaction has taken place, and many – if not most – are unfamiliar with what an ESOP is. Therefore, in this first communication, some companies choose to clarify that the business is now employee-owned and that there has not been a sale of the business to private equity or a strategic buyer. Often, this first communication is made via e-mail or company intranet, although it is, of course, up to the company to determine what method of communication works best within the organization.

Then, as soon as practical after the initial announcement – usually within one week to six months after ESOP implementation – there is a formal meeting to roll out the ESOP to employees. Generally, all employees who will be participants are invited to this formal rollout. Other possible attendees include parties involved with the company's ESOP process, such as the attorney; the ESOP Trustee (Trustee); representatives from the valuation firm, investment banking firm, and plan administrator; and members of the company's Board of Directors (Board). Sometimes, companies invite a consultant who specializes in employee communications to help relay the ESOP message to employees. A representative of another ESOP company may also make an appearance at the rollout to communicate their company's experience with the ESOP process.

At the formal rollout meeting, the company provides its staff with details about what an ESOP is and what it will mean for the employees. Typically, the first speaker at the formal rollout is the selling shareholder(s), who often explains why the ESOP was implemented. Reasons for choosing an ESOP over alternative ownership transition strategies are unique to each company; however, in our experience, sellers often mention how important the staff has been to the success of the company and the importance of the employees sharing in the company's success; a desire to continue the company's culture and values; the sellers' desire to transition to retirement; and the fact that the ESOP is a way to ensure the company will continue for generations.

The ESOP rollout meeting typically includes a formal introduction to the ESOP Trustee, at which time the Trustee will address the employees and explain their role during the transaction as well as on an ongoing basis. Other meeting presenters may include any of the aforementioned individuals.

PRAIRIE Pointer

Another important part of the formal rollout meeting is explaining to employees some of the specifics related to the ESOP, including the fact that the ESOP is a retirement plan; how employees become eligible to participate in the ESOP; how and when shares will be allocated to individual employee accounts; how the vesting process works; and what events would trigger a payout of a participant's ESOP stock. In many cases, companies also provide employees with a summary plan description (SPD) at the rollout meeting, or if the SPD is not yet complete, companies can provide a handout which summarizes the basics of the ESOP and informs employees that the SPD will be provided at a later date.

We have also found that, in order to avoid misunderstandings, it can be beneficial to explain what the ESOP does *not* mean for employees. For example, the hierarchy of the corporation and its authority and chain of command remains the same after the transaction. Therefore, although a trust now owns the shares of the company on behalf of the employees, implementation of the ESOP does not mean that employees get to make hiring and firing decisions. Ownership and management are separate, just like in publicly-traded companies. Similarly, employee ownership does not mean that employees have access to all of the company's financial information.

Participants have the right to read and review the ESOP plan and trust document. As a result, the company needs to make a copy of the plan and trust agreement available for review by participants, if requested.

Once all of this information is presented to the employees, they often have many questions which can be answered during a question and answer (Q&A) session, which usually occurs toward the end of the formal rollout meeting. There are some commonly-asked questions the seller and management may want to be prepared to answer at the Q&A session including:

- How much did the company sell for?
- How much is the business worth?
- How and when will I get my shares?
- When do I get vested in my account and how do I get paid?
- Does this affect my other forms of compensation? (i.e. 401(k), the cash bonus program, profit sharing)

In our experience, at nearly every rollout meeting, an employee will ask how much the company sold for and, usually, the seller does not want to answer this question. If this is not a question the seller wants to answer directly, they may instead want to assure the employees that the company sold for a fair price, but not more than a fair price, and that the Trustee, the independent financial advisor, and legal counsel looked over the transaction to ensure

---

One of Prairie's craft brewing clients held its ESOP rollout at the company's annual meeting.

The company's ESOP rollout incorporated terminology specific to the brewing industry in order to be relatable to employees. Phrases such as "crafting the future," "planting roots," and "letting it age" were used to describe how the ESOP works. The brewer also introduced a new craft beer at the rollout and staff was given the chance to name the beer to commemorate their ownership in the company.

that it was equitable for all parties involved. In addition, the U.S. Department of Labor (DOL) has the authority to review the transaction at any point within the following seven years.

In terms of the setting for the formal rollout meeting, there are many options. For example, some companies hold the rollout meeting during the workday, while others hold the rollout before or after the workday. We have also had clients who introduce the ESOP at their annual company meeting or make the rollout a special event or celebration. Regardless of which type of setting is chosen, it is important to keep in mind that the main goal of the rollout is employee communication.

Notably, companies that have multiple shifts, multiple locations, or both, will need to devise a way to allow all employees to attend the formal rollout meeting. Sometimes this involves solutions such as holding multiple meetings in the same day to accommodate shift workers or the use of technology such as online meeting software or video conferencing to enable remote office participation. The same idea holds true for companies that have a multilingual employee base. It is not uncommon for ESOP rollout meetings to have interpreters available to ensure that all employees have an opportunity to receive the message.

Also, the company should plan to hold an additional rollout meeting as soon as possible for those employees who were not able to attend the initial meeting. Many companies also record and archive the contents of the rollout meeting for future reference and for presentation to new employees.

As we discuss in more detail throughout this book, following the initial rollout, it is important for company management, human resources, and the ESOP Communications Committee (see Chapter 7 for further detail on ESOP Communications Committees) to work together to provide ESOP participants with additional education and messaging regarding the ESOP. Consistent and repeated communication regarding the ESOP is an essential component of a successful ESOP, as employee engagement and excitement about the ESOP can help promote revenue growth and profitability, resulting in lower employee turnover and enabling other important corporate objectives to be met.

Finally, company management should consider the possibility that some employees may initially be resistant to or cynical about the idea of an ESOP. In fact, they may believe that it sounds "too good to be true." One way to address this type of response is to have a clear initial message and then provide additional education so these employees understand that the ESOP is truly a benefit that enables them to help create value. One note of caution, however: in some cases, it may take time for employees to see that the ESOP is a meaningful benefit, and that may not occur until they see the value of their ESOP account significantly increase on their ESOP statement or when a co-worker leaves the company and gets a sizeable distribution from the ESOP. As the saying goes, "seeing is believing." Our experience is that ESOP naysayers can turn into some of the best ESOP advocates once they understand the true benefits of employee ownership.

CHAPTER 2

ESOP Stock:
Who Gets It? What Happens to It? And, How Do Participants Get Paid?

OFTENTIMES, the creation of an ESOP is the first ownership transition in a company's history. It is an exciting time for everyone involved, and plan participants will be eager to learn more about their new role as employee-owners.

As mentioned in Chapter 1, one of the first questions often asked by employees during the ESOP rollout meeting is "How do I get paid?" This chapter, which is broken down into three segments – Who Gets the ESOP Stock, What Happens to the ESOP Stock, and How Participants Get Paid – should help the company's management team answer that popular question.

Who Gets the ESOP Stock

The company's plan document sets the criteria for how employees become eligible to receive ESOP stock, when they become eligible, and what formulas govern how the stock will be allocated to each participant.

At a minimum, federal law requires a company's ESOP to include employees who are 21 years or older; have worked for the company for at least one year; work at least 1,000 hours during the plan year; and are employed as of the last day of the plan year. While these regulations obligate ESOP companies to comply with these minimum standards, ESOP companies can choose to make the eligibility requirements for their ESOP "better" or "more generous" than the minimum standards – keeping in mind that they cannot reverse such a decision and make the eligibility requirements "worse" or "less generous" at some point in the future without good reason. For instance, depending on the demographics of their employees or the seasonality of their business, a company may choose to lower the minimum age requirement for participation from 21 to 18 years of age and the minimum hour requirement from 1,000 to 500. However, if those minimums are established, they cannot be reversed over the course of time to make the age or minimum hour requirements higher without a valid reason. Even if the company has a good reason for changing the ESOP eligibility requirements, the minimums must still comply with federal guidelines.

With regard to how much stock will be given to each participant, most companies set up the allocation formula in proportion to the participants' salaries. This allocation formula is referred to as "pro rata compensation." For example, if a participant's salary is 3% of the total qualified payroll in a given year, that participant would receive 3% of the ESOP stock that is allocated during that year. However, a few companies have more advanced allocation formulas which, for example, may take into account other factors,

PRAIRIE Pointer

such as years of service. As is the case with other defined contribution plans – for example, a 401(k) plan – the amount of individual compensation that "counts" in the typical allocation formulas is capped and reset each year based on a cost of living adjustment.

Regardless, after the ESOP has been in place for some time, the Board may decide to revisit the issue of eligibility in order to ensure that the company is delivering the benefits of the ESOP to employees in a way that is consistent with the company's goals. For example, we have found that, after the company begins to pay off the ESOP debt, the Board sometimes becomes more willing to relax the eligibility requirements and allow employees to participate in the plan sooner than the plan initially provided. Or, if the company begins to operate overseas after the ESOP is in place, although the company's international employees generally do not qualify for participation in an ESOP established in the U.S., there are mechanisms the company can employ to set up a plan that mimics the U.S. ESOP. (We recommend that you check with your advisors and legal counsel for further details if this is something the company wishes to do.)

If the seller of the company has elected tax deferral under Internal Revenue Code Section 1042 and continues to work as an officer of the company after the ESOP is implemented, the seller and any of his/her direct lineal descendants may be precluded from participating in the ESOP. For more specific detail and to explore other options for the seller, we recommend consulting with your advisors.

What Happens to the ESOP Stock

When the ESOP is implemented, the ESOP trust consists of individual accounts for each eligible plan participant. These trust accounts hold the shares of stock that are allocated to the participants each year, as well as any cash or investments that have been allocated to the participants. Depending on the share price and changes in the cash balances in the accounts, the value of each participant's account can fluctuate. So that participants are aware of the value of their account, the company is required to provide each participant with an ESOP statement every year. This statement gives participants information that, at a minimum, conveys (1) the number of shares in the account, (2) the value per share, (3) the amount of any cash in the account, and (4) to what percent the employee is vested.

Notably, participants may not be fully vested in the ESOP immediately – that is, as with many other retirement benefits, the participant may need to remain employed by the company for a specified number of years before being entitled to receive the full value of their ESOP shares when their employment is terminated. For the ESOP company, vesting is a way to incentivize employees to remain at the company. Each year, the participant becomes more fully vested – or gains an irrevocable right to a larger percentage of the ESOP stock in their account – until the time they are 100% vested. Once that happens, if the participant leaves the company, they are entitled to receive the full benefit of all shares in their account. If, however, the participant leaves the company before being fully vested, they forfeit the portion of the benefit which is not yet fully vested.

There are different ways companies can approach vesting. One option is cliff vesting, which requires the participant to remain employed at the company for a prescribed amount of time – no more than three years – before they become vested at all; after the prescribed amount of time, the participant immediately becomes fully vested. So, if they leave before the set time, they receive no benefit.

More commonly, ESOP companies employ graded vesting, which is when the participant becomes vested in a percentage of the ESOP each year over the course of no more than six years total. With graded vesting, the participant must be at least 20% vested after two years of participation and then will become at least 20% vested each year for the following four years. Of course, these are the minimum prescribed terms for graded vesting; a company can choose to award vesting at a faster pace. For instance, at some companies, participants are fully vested after five years, during which time they earn 20% vesting each year. Regardless of the pace, if graded vesting is used, participants who leave the company before they are fully vested relinquish their right to receive any part of the benefit which is not vested. So, if a participant leaves the company when they are only 40% vested, they forfeit the remaining 60% of their account balance. There is, however, an exception to this rule if the participant dies or becomes disabled.

Moreover, as with any other investment, diversification is an important issue within the context of ESOPs. In general, diversification of investments is vital to mitigate the risk of having a large amount of one's net worth concentrated in just one type of stock. However, when a participant holds shares in an ESOP of a privately-held company, the value of the shares is exclusively tied to the value of the company. Due to the risk that comes with having retirement funds locked up in a single, privately-held, non-marketable security, once a participant reaches the age of 55 and has completed at least 10 years of participation in the ESOP, federal regulations give the participant the option to diversify up to 25% of the shares allocated to their account. Therefore, if something negative were to happen to the value of the ESOP stock close to, or at, the participant's retirement date, there is less risk that the participant will experience a significant loss in the value of their retirement benefit. Then, when that participant reaches age 60, they are given a set timeframe within which they can choose to diversify up to 50% of their stock balance. Companies have the option to offer more generous diversification guidelines, but at a minimum, they must comply with these rules. For further guidance, consult your plan document and your trusted advisor.

How Participants Get Paid

When an ESOP participant leaves the company – whether due to retirement, death, disability, or other employment – or when the participant diversifies their account, the company must fund the repurchase of the participant's shares at fair market value. This transaction can happen either at one time or over a period of time, depending on the details outlined in the plan document.

At the same time, federal regulations outline some baseline requirements regarding distributions. If the termination of employment is a result of disability, death, or merely the fact that the participant has reached normal retirement age, distributions are required to start during the plan year immediately following termination. Meanwhile, if the termination results from the participant's resignation or firing, distributions must begin no later than six years after the plan year during which the participant left.

Distributions may be made either in a lump sum or over the course of time. Sometimes, plan documents prescribe a certain method of distribution depending on the situation. For instance, a company may choose to give a lump sum in cases of death or disability but choose distribution of equal installment payments over five years in the case of retirement. Regardless, if the company pays over time, the payments must be made at least annually and over the course of no more than five years. Further, the company can always amend the distribution policies outlined in their plan document, as long as the company is making the policy better

PRAIRIE Pointer

for the participants instead of worse, as previously discussed.

In any case, the distribution timeline should follow the plan document and should be as consistent as possible from year to year.

There are pros and cons to both types of distribution, and each company must decide what works best for them. For example, by paying a lump sum, the company could be required to distribute a significant amount of money all at one time, whereas with a payout over time, the company can better regulate their cash flow. On the other hand, paying via a lump sum may be beneficial to the company if they anticipate that the share value will increase quickly over the course of a five-year payout; the company may end up disbursing far less by paying a lump sum at the current year's share price than they would over the course of the following years if the stock price increases.

Notably, if the ESOP is paying off a loan used to buy company shares, distribution to participants may be delayed until after the loan is repaid. This is due to the fact that, if the company started paying participants who leave the company while they are still paying off the ESOP loan, it could be detrimental to the company's cash flow.

Once all ESOP shares are allocated, the company needs to make a choice: 1) do nothing at all; 2) issue more shares; 3) put cash in ESOP accounts in lieu of stock; or 4) a combination of options (2) and (3). Otherwise, there may not be an additional retirement benefit. The company should consult their trusted advisors to plan for how to approach this issue before the ESOP shares are fully allocated and run out.

Regardless of the form of the payout, participants' distributions will be made in one of three ways: a check, a rollover into the 401(k) at the participant's new place of employment, or a rollover into a self-directed individual retirement account. ESOP companies should make outgoing participants aware of the fact that receiving a check could come with hefty tax penalties that a rollover would not.

One important item to note is that, unlike some other retirement plans, ESOPs typically do not allow for borrowing against funds or the early withdrawal of funds. The exception to this rule is when a participant wishes to make a hardship withdrawal. For instance, if the participant has $100,000 worth of medical bills, $10,000 in their bank savings account, and $200,000 in their ESOP account, the participant may apply for a hardship withdrawal from the ESOP, if the company allows.

CHAPTER 3

The Rights of ESOP Participants

ESOP participants are guaranteed a number of rights under the law, many of which require that companies provide participants with information about the ESOP. A company's legal counsel can help provide further details regarding the totality of an ESOP participants' rights. However, following is a list of some of these rights.

- *Summary Plan Description* – Within 90 days of becoming a participant, an ESOP company's employees are entitled to receive an SPD, which clearly outlines important details regarding the plan, such as when an employee is eligible to participate in the ESOP, vesting rights, when a participant is entitled to a distribution from the ESOP, when the plan's year ends, participant voting rights, and the names and addresses of the plan sponsor and the plan fiduciaries. Many of the best SPDs that we have seen are not overly technical and are written in a Q&A format. If amendments are made to the plan document, the SPD may also need to be updated and distributed to participants.

- *Participant Benefit Statements* – Participants must receive an annual statement indicating the fair market value of their shares as well as any other assets – such as cash – in the ESOP. The statement should also indicate the degree to which the participant is vested in their shares of the ESOP. The participant statement is typically prepared by the plan administrator and, like many other retirement benefit statements, allows the participant to track the changes to their account from the beginning of the plan year to the end of the plan year.

- *Summary Annual Report* – For ESOPs with a December 31st year-end, by July 31st of the following year, or October 15th if an extension is filed, the company must complete a summary annual report on Form 5500, which includes information about plan activity and assets. Not only must ESOP participants be able to view the report, but they are also entitled to receive a shortened version of the company's Form 5500.

- *Access to Plan Documents* – Participants have the right to read and review the plan document, any trust documents, and the ESOP's most recent annual report. In order to facilitate this, companies may consider instituting a library system, as part of which participants can check out the document(s) to be reviewed and check them back in when the review is complete.

- *Participant Voting Rights* – Although they are not extensive, ESOP participants have some voting rights in relation to certain specific and significant events. For example, ESOP participants in private companies have the right to direct the ESOP Trustee on how to vote the ESOP stock when all, or substantially all, of the company's assets are to be sold. When this type of pass-through vote is required, the participants are entitled to receive a mailing containing information regarding the issue to be voted upon by the Trustee. (It is important to note that ESOP participants generally do not have the right to direct the Trustee on votes regarding a sale of the company's stock.)

This list is not all-inclusive, and companies can structure their plans to exceed the minimum degree of participant rights.

PART 2

Who Does What?

CHAPTER 4

Board of Directors

Section 1 – Board of Directors Overview

Before selling to an ESOP, many companies are founder- or family-run businesses with a Board that is quite small, often consisting solely of the company's shareholder(s) or family and friends. In addition, many Boards fail to hold formal meetings on a regular basis or take formal minutes of the meetings.

However, once an ESOP is put in place, the size of the Board and the manner in which the Board operates will likely need to change – sometimes significantly. For instance, not only will the Board need to satisfy any size requirements that the ESOP Trustee may have included in the transaction documents, but also, the members of the Board will need to ensure that they are taking steps to fulfill their fiduciary duties, namely the duty of care and the duty of loyalty.

In general terms, the fiduciary duty of care requires a board member to be informed regarding all material information that is reasonably available to them before making a business decision and to use the amount of care that a prudent person would use in similar circumstances. Meanwhile, the duty of loyalty relates to fiduciaries' conflicts of interest; it requires that board members put the company's interests above their own. Examples of violations of the duty of loyalty include the misuse of corporate assets or opportunities, fraud, bad faith, or self-dealing.

Notably, board members owe their fiduciary duties exclusively to the shareholders, which, in the case of a 100% ESOP, is the ESOP Trust. (Participants in the ESOP are beneficial owners of the stock, but the Trust itself is the legal shareholder.) Moreover, in the few – but growing – number of ESOP-owned public benefit corporations (also known as B corporations), depending on the company's charter, board members may also be required to take into account the public good as well as the shareholders' interests when making decisions regarding the company.

In any case, the board members of an ESOP company must keep these fiduciary duties in mind when carrying out their numerous responsibilities, which include – but are not limited to – the following:

- Establishing the strategic vision and direction of the company
- Reviewing management's long-term plan for consistency with the strategic plan as well as management's ability to execute the plan
- Hiring and, if necessary, firing the Chief Executive Officer (CEO)
- Advising the CEO and helping to set his/her strategic goals
- Establishing corporate policies
- Setting compensation policies for the CEO and possibly the senior management team
- Evaluating changes to the company's marketing plan

PRAIRIE Pointer

- Monitoring the company's financial performance and reviewing financial statements

- Reviewing and approving financial audits and the company's budget(s)

- Securing adequate funding for the organization

- Evaluating significant corporate transactions, including offers to purchase the company

- Ensuring a succession plan is in place for the CEO and key members of senior management

- Approving contracts, as appropriate

- Appointing members to the Board's committees (and sub-committees, if there are any)

- Hiring a qualified plan administrator

- Hiring a qualified ESOP Trustee and monitoring the ESOP Trustee's performance

- Replacing the ESOP Trustee when necessary

- Planning for repurchase obligation and sustainability

- Determining contributions to the ESOP and other qualified plans

> The ESOP company's Board should focus on establishing the strategic vision for the company, not day-to-day operations; that work should be left to the company's management team.

Further, once an ESOP is implemented, there are several issues the company must address, including the size of the Board (if this has not already been addressed in the transaction documents). We have found that it is best for a Board to have an uneven number of members so that there are no ties when votes are taken. For most mid-size ESOP companies, the Board consists of three to five members, with five members being the ideal board size. In our experience, once the number of board members rises above seven, it can become logistically difficult for a Board to accomplish its goals.

In terms of the composition of the Board, even if the selling shareholder is no longer the company's CEO once the ESOP is implemented, he/she typically remains on the Board as long as he/she is still involved with the company. In any case, the company's CEO is generally a board member. With regard to other members of the management team, in terms of frequency, we have noticed it is most common for the senior management in both operations and finance to be on the Board of the typical mid-sized ESOP company.

Additionally, it is increasingly common for the ESOP Trustee to require independent members to join the Board. This type of board member is not personally or professionally affiliated with the company itself and may offer a unique perspective or different expertise than board members that come from within the company. Typically, in a mid-size company, the ESOP Trustee will request the addition of between one and three independent board members. Ideally, independent members should fit with the company's culture, have an understanding of the organization's key priorities, have skills that are complementary to the company's business or needs, and be independent enough to speak up and add value while exercising impartial judgment.

While adding independent board members can be very beneficial, companies may find that it is difficult to find people willing to serve as an independent board member. One reason for this difficulty

PRAIRIE Pointer

is that board members can be at risk of litigation if they fail to fulfill their fiduciary duties of care and loyalty. This risk dissuades some individuals from agreeing to serve as an independent board member. Although the company will invest in directors and officers liability insurance to help protect the independent board member(s), in light of the risk of personal liability, companies will also need to compensate independent board members.

The type of compensation given to independent board members varies by company, although typically, independent members are compensated for attending board meetings and committee meetings as well as for phone calls. In our experience, the amount of compensation depends on factors such as the size and complexity of the company. For example, an independent board member of a company with $50 million in revenue might receive a $15,000 to $20,000 stipend, whereas an independent board member of a company with $2 billion in revenue may be paid $50,000 to $100,000.

In large part, the type of candidate that makes a good independent board member depends on the particular needs of the company and the skill set of those already on the Board. For example, many companies want the independent board

Interestingly, the Board appoints the ESOP Trustee while the ESOP Trustee votes to appoint the Board. In light of this circularity, the ESOP Trustee will generally not be on the Board because this could lead to a conflict of interest. The Trustee's primary responsibility is to act in the best interest of the shareholders, whereas the Board may be in conflict. It may be difficult for the Trustee to fulfill their fiduciary duties to the participants if faced with this type of situation.

members to have a thorough understanding of their business; therefore, they look for respected, often retired, individuals from their own industry. These people understand what the company does, have familiarity with the company's capital structure, and know the industry, which can be very helpful not only to current board members but also to future board members.

Meanwhile, some companies search for an individual that has an understanding of how ESOPs work. These people can serve as a sounding board for some of the ESOP-related issues that come up regularly and provide guidance to the other members of the Board.

In other cases, a company may be planning to make acquisitions, so they look for an independent board member that has a financial background. So, for example, the company may seek someone who was a Chief Financial Officer (CFO) for a company that made many acquisitions or an investment banker that has knowledge of mergers and acquisitions.

Notably, there are various ways to find someone to serve as an independent board member, such as asking professional contacts (e.g. the ESOP Trustee, corporate counsel, the valuation firm, owners of other businesses in the industry) for recommendations; contacting relevant industry associations; or, in the case of larger companies, utilizing an executive search firm.

Since it can be difficult to find independent board members, the ESOP Trustee will give the company some time to find them. You can expect the search to take several months to a full year, especially if more than one independent board member is required.

Once the potential members of the Board have been identified, the slate of board members – both internal and independent – must be submitted to the ESOP Trustee to be vetted and, later, for a vote. In a 100% ESOP-owned company, the Trustee votes on behalf of the ESOP for all of the board members. However, prior to

PRAIRIE Pointer

voting, the Trustee will likely want to review the resume of any candidate(s) for independent board member(s) and, in some cases, may want to interview the candidate(s) in order to learn about their qualifications and whether they are truly independent. When voting, the Trustee can dismiss a potential board member from the slate. (Incidentally, the Trustee can – at any time, not just when voting on the annual slate – remove a board member for failure to fulfill their fiduciary duties or because they are otherwise ineffective.) Notably, in some cases, Boards have staggered terms for their members, so every board member may not be subject to a Trustee vote at the same time.

Moreover, according to the National Center for Employee Ownership (NCEO), there is a consensus that ESOP Boards should be more active than Boards at private, non-ESOP companies. As a result, Boards for ESOP companies need to meet regularly. Typically, meetings are held quarterly. The Board should set a formal agenda for each meeting, and minutes of the meeting should be taken and approved at the next board meeting. Topics discussed during board meetings may include any of the items listed previously as part of the Board's responsibilities.

> To determine what skills to look for in an independent board member, the best practice is to establish a Board level "scorecard" to inventory the skill sets already represented on the Board and to then search for independent members whose skills either fill a gap or add needed depth.

Additionally, the Board will need to establish several committees, including the following essential committees:

- *Audit Committee* – This committee has responsibility for the company's financial reporting, including setting accounting policies, hiring and monitoring the company's auditors, as well as regulatory compliance and certain aspects of financial risk management.

- *Compensation Committee* – This committee has responsibility for setting total compensation for the senior executives of the company as well as company policies about pay. In addition to salary, policies on pay may include other items such as stock, phantom stock, stock appreciation rights, bonuses, profit sharing, etc.

In terms of the structure of these committees, it is a best practice for the chair of both the audit and compensation committees to be an independent board member. In addition, if there are at least two independent board members, it is very common for one to chair the audit committee and the other to chair the compensation committee and for both to serve on whichever of these committees they do not chair. The reason for this is to ensure that appropriate questions are asked of the outside audit firm, the CFO, etc., and to ensure that the committee is fully briefed. For example, if the company has a handful of bad receivables, the independent board member should ask the CFO to explain the company's major receivables and how the bad receivables are impacting the company's profit and loss statement.

As far as committee members from the company, the audit committee usually includes the CEO and CFO. If the CFO is on the not on the Board, the committee will undoubtedly consult with the CFO regarding any questions that arise. The compensation committee may also include the CEO.

Other possible committees that may be formed by the Board include:

- ESOP Administrative Committee, which oversees day-to-day operations of the ESOP and is discussed in detail later in this chapter
- Nominating Committee, which is in charge of nominating directors or the slate of directors
- Ethics Committee, which sets guidelines for ethics and standards
- Executive Committee, which includes the officers of the Board and oversees the execution of the Board's duties

There may also be special purpose committees established for specific one-time issues that the Board may have to evaluate.

Section 2 – The Evolution of the ESOP: Repurchase Obligation and Sustainability

One of the Board's many responsibilities is planning for repurchase obligation.

When an ESOP participant in a closely-held company retires, is terminated, becomes disabled, or dies, the company – not the ESOP Trustee – is legally obligated to fund the departing participant's stock repurchase at its current fair market value; this is known as repurchase obligation.

In general, the amount of a company's repurchase obligation has to do with factors such as the demographics of the company's employees; the percentage to which departing participants are vested; the ESOP stock price; participants' diversification rights; and the plan's payout requirements (when ESOP distributions must begin, if they are to be made in a lump sum or over time, etc.). In addition, repurchase obligation can include other long-term liabilities of the company such as stock appreciation rights (SARs) or any other synthetic equity plan granted to the management team.

Notably, repurchase obligation is not typically a high priority for companies with newly-installed ESOPs because the perception is that the first payout from the ESOP will not occur for many years. Additionally, during the first few years after an ESOP is implemented, most companies are highly leveraged and are instead focused on paying down the debt that was incurred to finance the ESOP. However, as the value of the ESOP shares grows during subsequent years, the amount of repurchase obligation will also rise.

If the Board does not properly plan for repurchase obligation, it can become increasingly burdensome for the company to manage. As is the case with many financial planning decisions, it is imperative that the Board act sooner rather than later. Indeed, experts suggest that a multitude of challenges can arise if an ESOP company does not have a plan to address its repurchase obligation, including devaluation of company stock; poor employee morale as a result of declining company stock values; a limited ability to secure corporate credit; personal liability for ESOP fiduciaries; and/or company insolvency created by the cash flow demands of repurchase obligation. As a result, a few years after an ESOP is implemented – if not sooner – the company's attention should shift from focusing exclusively on the payment of debt to also include planning for the payment of repurchase obligation and, longer-term, how to sustain the ESOP.

In our experience, many 100% ESOP-owned companies face a scenario similar to the following: Right after the ESOP is implemented, the equity value of the ESOP stock is depressed because of the loan debt the company incurred in order to start the ESOP. However, since the company is usually not paying taxes – for example, a 100% ESOP-owned S corporation (S-corp)

PRAIRIE Pointer

generally has no federal income tax liability – they use much of the cash they would have otherwise used for taxes to pay off their ESOP loan, which, in turn, results in significant deleveraging. Concurrently, the value of the equity increases, and as a result, the ESOP share value rises. Oftentimes, during the first few years of the ESOP, the company experiences rapid growth in equity, causing the value of the ESOP shares to increase very quickly; in fact, it is not unusual for a company to experience a super-normal return on equity during this period. Nevertheless, this type of increase in the value of the ESOP stock does not generally continue over the long-term; the amount that the ESOP stock increases typically slows once the loan debt is repaid. Still, the stock value can increase further – although usually not as rapidly as it did during the first few years of the ESOP, depending on how profitable the company is once it is no longer paying the loan; the absence of the loan allows many companies to build up their cash reserves since that cash is no longer needed to pay off debt. Notably, the cumulative impact of retaining cash on the balance sheet year after year can result in a significant increase in the value of the company, as well as the ESOP stock value, and in turn, the amount of repurchase obligation.

Although the Board needs to plan for repurchase obligation, typically, since it is a contingent liability, repurchase obligation is not required to be included on the company's balance sheet. Therefore, the company's management team must be vigilant about developing a plan to account for this liability and seek support from the Board and its ESOP advisors for implementation of that plan. The management team should monitor the plan and make course corrections as needed.

One way to plan for the liability associated with repurchase obligation is to obtain a repurchase obligation study. Most providers of repurchase obligation studies are plan administrators that offer a repurchase obligation study software package.

In general terms, a repurchase obligation study makes a long-term projection of the number of shares the company will need to repurchase over time and the corresponding cost to the company. More specifically, the repurchase obligation study is an actuarial analysis, and the firm performing the study may review variables such as who works at the company; employees' ages and tenure; the estimated number of people who will likely retire in the next year, two years, five years, 10 years, etc.; the amount of stock the participants are expected to own when they leave; the estimated shares that will be elected for diversification; and more. To do so, the repurchase obligation study folds in the plan dynamics – how much stock will likely be allocated every year and how much the shares will be worth every year on a long-term basis. The study then assigns a dollar amount per year that it expects the company will need in order to pay for the stock of those participants who are no longer part of the ESOP.

Notably, we have found that, depending on the size and characteristics of the original ESOP transaction, some lenders require a repurchase obligation study to be conducted prior to implementation of the ESOP. However, this is somewhat rare. In cases where a repurchase obligation study is not done before the transaction, the best practice is to do one no later than three years into the ESOP. Thereafter, the study should be updated every three to five years, or more often if there are significant changes to the company's performance, the corporate structure, or the terms of the plan.

PRAIRIE Pointer

While a quality estimate of the required number of future share purchases can be developed by a thorough analysis of actuarial data, in our experience, oftentimes, the estimates of share price appreciation included in repurchase obligation studies are loosely developed and do not incorporate the methodologies utilized by ESOP appraisers. Inappropriate estimates of share price appreciation can significantly affect the quality of the repurchase obligation study which can, in turn, lead the company to make poor business decisions. For example, inaccurate share price assumptions can cause the company to either over- or underfund the reserves it sets aside for future repurchase obligation, which can impact the financial health of the business. Also, inaccurate share price assumptions may impact the company's annual ESOP valuation, as ESOP appraisers utilize this output when conducting the annual valuation.

In order to plan more effectively, we recommend that companies ask the firm conducting their repurchase obligation study to team up with a valuation firm who can provide a better understanding of cash flow related to operating expenses and long-term business strategies as well as provide a more accurate value trajectory, thus increasing the usefulness of the repurchase obligation study. Additionally, a valuation

Independent trustees and fiduciaries generally require that repurchase obligation be addressed as part of the annual ESOP valuation.

firm can give the company advice as to how to manage repurchase obligation as part of a sustainability analysis – and this can be especially important since there may be an entirely different stock price trajectory if the company is managing to the benefit level it wants to provide to its employees. Managing to the benefit level is something we highly recommend. In our experience, companies who do not manage to the benefit level often have difficulty keeping the benefit level stable, and that can ultimately impact the value of the company as well as the sustainability of both the company and the ESOP.

In any case, when it is time for the company to repurchase participant shares, the company will need to determine the repurchase method it will employ. The company has several options it can use to convert participants' shares from stock to cash. The most common options utilized are "recycling" and "redeeming." Recycling involves the contribution of cash to the ESOP by the company, which the ESOP distributes to the participant in exchange for their stock. With recycling, the shares remain in the trust and are reallocated among the remaining participants in the plan. On the other hand, when redeeming, the company buys back the participant's shares either from the participant – after they have been distributed – or from the ESOP directly. In the latter case, the ESOP will distribute cash in lieu of stock to the participant. In either event, when shares are redeemed, they are put into the company's treasury, which reduces the number of outstanding shares.

It is important to note that a company's decision about the method(s) by which shares are repurchased can change each year, and a combination of methods can be chosen to target a specific benefit level. At the same time, we have found that every decision a Board makes about repurchase obligation affects every future decision about repurchase obligation as well as the value of the ESOP stock. Oftentimes, repurchase obligation decisions made

PRAIRIE Pointer

toward the beginning of the ESOP can significantly affect the share price of the company over the 10, 20, 30+ year trajectory. Also, how a company pays for repurchase obligation and what it does when repurchasing the stock affects every participant in the plan, as well as future participants – conceivably, for generations to come.

Therefore, to help prevent repurchase obligation issues from negatively impacting a company's future growth, the company should not only prepare for how to handle the company's repurchase obligation but also be thoughtful about the possible implications of current decisions on the future of the ESOP when planning how to deal with repurchase obligation. Additionally, it is imperative for the management team and the Board to become educated about repurchase obligation so that they understand it and are aware of its significance in the overall sustainability of the company and the ESOP.

In an ESOP-owned company, the concept of sustainability relates to perpetuating the ESOP while maintaining the health of the business. According to the NCEO, "A truly sustainable ESOP company…has a strategy to maintain an effective employee ownership culture and a profitable business model. In particular, this means effective leadership succession strategies,

The benefit level – which is typically communicated as a percentage of qualified payroll – is the rate at which contributions are made by the company to employee retirement plans. These contributions can take a variety of forms such as safe-harbor contributions made to a 401(k), ESOP loan amortization payments, and contributions directly to the ESOP. Benefit levels are set by the Board.

a governance structure consistent with employee ownership, having a strategy for sustained growth, and more." We believe it is important for ESOP Trustees and employee-owned companies to understand how the ESOP impacts their business in the short- and long-term and to develop a plan for the sustainable ESOP; this will enable confident decision-making.

The planning process for creating a sustainable ESOP company should begin with a high-level discussion that outlines the long-term objectives of the company. This discussion must address the company's business strategy, long-term growth objectives, and

Managing to the Benefit Level

An important part of managing repurchase obligation – as well as the sustainability of both the company and the ESOP – is managing to the retirement benefit level set by the company's Board. For example, if the Board indicates that the benefit level should not exceed a total of 9%, the company could choose to make a safe-harbor contribution to an employee's 401(k) plan equal to 3% of the employee's pay and a 6% contribution to the ESOP. This ESOP contribution can be used to pay the ESOP loan amortization, which is used to satisfy the ESOP loan; any excess cash can be used to satisfy repurchase obligation or may be invested in a broad basket of securities on behalf of the participants.

If, however, assuming these same facts, a group of participants who have substantial balances also terminate employment, resulting in a repurchase obligation that extends beyond the excess contribution, the company will need to decide how to deal with the shares which must be repurchased as a result of the terminations. In this case, the company does not need any more contributions to the ESOP to satisfy the employee benefit level. As a result, in order to remain at the 9% benefit level, the repurchased shares could be redeemed or funded through S-corp distributions to the ESOP.

It is important to recognize that the only way to provide retirement benefits via the ESOP is through making ESOP contributions. These contributions are allocated to participants based on their relative compensation in a manner outlined in the plan

targeted benefit levels, with the goal being the alignment of all of these considerations. Additionally, it should also anticipate the potential magnitude of the liability and its timing relative to other potentially significant cash needs such as seller note maturity, warrant realization, or SARs payouts. Many companies also find that, as part of this planning process, it is very helpful to have a sustainability study done by a valuation firm. Typically, sustainability studies are recommended every three to five years or whenever there is a significant change in the corporation – for example, a large capital expansion, potential acquisition, international

document. S-corp distributions track the shares rather than compensation; as such, funding repurchase obligation through this methodology will only enhance the value for the participants who have already received allocations. That said, there is one instance where S-corp distributions will be allocated to participants based on compensation. Should an S-corp distribution be made in an ESOP company that still has unallocated stock, the portion of the S-corp distribution associated with the unallocated shares will be allocated to participants based on the formula in the plan.

It is also important to note that, while a redemption strategy and an S-corp distribution strategy produce similar results as to how value is allocated to individual participants within the plan, some differences will exist if the company utilizes a synthetic equity plan. While the same level of cash will be required to satisfy the repurchase obligation under the redemption and S-corp distribution strategies, the resulting per-share price after the transactions will differ due to the variance in outstanding shares. As such, a redemption strategy will produce a higher per-share price which can affect the value of the synthetic equity plans which, in turn, reduces the value of individual ESOP accounts.

In essence, determining how to buy back shares in order to manage to the benefit level is algebraic and ongoing. In each case, the company needs to consider the inputs and make a decision to redeem stock and/or make S-corp distributions to recycle the shares accordingly.

expansion, or a significant change in employee demographics. In our experience, while it is beneficial to do a repurchase obligation study every three to five years, it is preferable to do a sustainability study every three to five years since the sustainability study will not only include a review of repurchase obligation, but it will also incorporate better valuation methodologies which will likely result in a more accurate forecast of share price appreciation, as discussed previously.

A sustainability study done by a valuation firm will review the company as a whole, and the valuation firm will work with the company through the ESOP Trustee to make a plan that supports both the company's and the ESOP's success.

While repurchase obligation certainly needs to be examined as part of a sustainability study since it can have a significant impact on the company, to build a sustainable ESOP, the planning process must be more comprehensive than just a forecast of the shares that will become eligible for repurchase. The study must also look at the interrelationship between repurchase obligation and valuation, the cash flow implications related to sponsoring the ESOP and how they affect other corporate objectives, as well as management succession.

Among other things, a sustainability study can include:

- Analysis of current and future employee benefit levels and whether these benefit levels can be maintained
- Analysis of the impact of capital spending
- Analysis of the company's ability to sustain a severe downturn
- Analysis of the company's ability to handle rapid growth
- Scenario tests that use different ESOP policy decisions
- Review of how ESOP policy can impact synthetic equity programs

ESOP Sustainability Variables

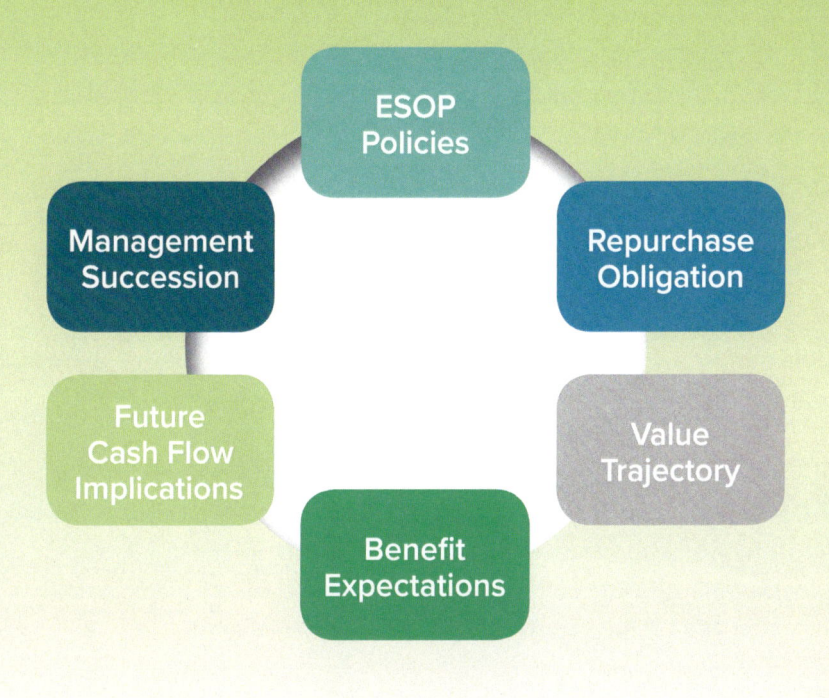

- ESOP Policies
- Repurchase Obligation
- Value Trajectory
- Benefit Expectations
- Future Cash Flow Implications
- Management Succession

- Plans to align policies with corporate strategic goals
- Forecasts of future share price trajectories under different scenarios
- Review of the company's management succession plan

Based on the valuation firm's analysis of these and other factors, the company should come to understand how it can make decisions about ESOP policies, corporate governance, and leadership development to influence an optimized, sustainable outcome for both the company and the ESOP.

Section 3 – ESOP Administration Committee

As mentioned previously, the Board has the opportunity to create several committees to assist in their duties. The ESOP Administration Committee is one such committee. Since this type of committee is involved in the day-to-day operations of the ESOP, an ESOP Administration Committee can serve as a valuable liaison to the Board on any issue regarding the administration of the ESOP. Notably, there is no legal requirement to have an ESOP Administration Committee; however, because of the value it can bring to the Board, oftentimes, a directive to create such a committee is outlined in the plan document.

If the Board decides to form an ESOP Administration Committee, or if the plan document requires it, the Board will typically appoint three to six members to serve on the committee. Sometimes the plan document requires a specific number of members, so it is important to check your plan. These members can be a combination of board members and members of the company's management team; however, some companies have no board members at all on their ESOP Administration Committee. In some situations, one or more of the company's non-management employees are elected or appointed to the ESOP Administration Committee as well. Regardless, having non-board members on the ESOP Administration Committee tends to help focus board members on the fact that the company is an employee-owned business.

With regard to the specific duties of the ESOP Administration Committee, overseeing the administration of the ESOP and its operations is the committee's primary duty. While the committee will not administer the plan itself – that is the responsibility of the plan administrator (as discussed more fully in Section 4 of this chapter) – the ESOP Administration Committee is there to ensure that the plan administrator is doing its job. Namely, the committee

PRAIRIE Pointer

will confirm that participant statements are delivered promptly, that participants are paid, and that allocations are properly made. Moreover, the ESOP Administration Committee may be responsible for the following duties:

- Directing the Trustee on plan decisions, such as voting shares
- Making recommendations to the Board regarding the hiring and firing of the Trustee and other service providers
- Reviewing the performance of the Trustee
- Choosing and/or changing the plan administrator and reviewing their performance
- Managing plan assets
- Making decisions on plan design and amendments to the plan document
- Overseeing repurchase obligation studies and implementing plans to deal with any issues that arise from the studies

An ESOP Administration Committee can actually serve as the Trustee of the ESOP; however, most committees only serve in an advisory capacity.

In addition to assuming some or all of these duties, another significant reason for appointing an ESOP Administration Committee focuses around receipt of the valuation report. The Trustee is responsible for engaging the valuation firm, so the valuation report is officially the sole property of the Trustee. The Trustee is only obligated to share the per-share stock price with the Board and the plan administrator in the form of a letter; the Trustee is not required to provide the Board or the plan administrator with a copy of the full valuation report. Oftentimes, boards are frustrated by the idea of not being able to get a copy of the valuation report. If that is the case, the Board should establish a formal ESOP Administration Committee, as the Trustee generally will provide a copy of the valuation report to the committee upon request.

Notably, depending on what decisions the ESOP Administration Committee makes and what their actions are, individuals on the committee may have a fiduciary duty. In these cases, the ESOP Administration Committee would be legally responsible for the operation of the ESOP. Some of the actions that would result in committee members assuming a fiduciary duty include making decisions or giving direction regarding:

- Management of plan assets
- Buying or selling stock
- Investing assets in employer stock and other investments or moving ESOP assets to another plan
- Voting of shares when a pass-through vote is not required
- Ensuring that the ESOP pays no more than fair market value for repurchased ESOP stock
- Ensuring that the ESOP operation and design complies with the Employee Retirement Income Security Act of 1974 (ERISA), which governs ESOPs
- Selecting qualified advisors

It is often the case that company employees, even senior management, have little practical experience in these subjects. If members of the ESOP Administration Committee feel uncomfortable making decisions on these types of issues, care must be taken. The company should consider bringing in an independent fiduciary or Trustee if internally trusteed; however, if directing an external Trustee or fiduciary, the company should consider relinquishing the internal Trustee role and granting discretionary power to an external party. In either case, though, the Board needs to approve of these actions.

In comparison, other committee actions, such as changing plan features in compliance with ERISA; terminating the plan; voting for the Board; setting benefit levels; and any other general administration of the plan, may not be considered fiduciary in nature. Regardless of what type of decision they make, ESOP Administration Committee members should use prudence and care.

Section 4 – ESOP Plan Administrator

In light of the complexity associated with the administration of an ESOP, an experienced, qualified ESOP plan administrator is an important partner to the ESOP-owned company. A plan administrator is not only responsible for all recordkeeping and reporting requirements related to the ESOP but also oversees the operations of the ESOP; as part of this oversight, the plan administrator allocates participant shares, determines the percentage to which participants are vested in the plan, tracks each participant's account value, and more. The purpose of the Board employing a professional plan administrator – a third-party firm that is independent from the company – is to ensure that the plan document is interpreted properly and benefits are given to participants consistent with the terms of the ESOP.

One of the primary responsibilities of the plan administrator is to issue annual statements to the ESOP participants. These statements

PRAIRIE Pointer

The term "plan administrator" can be used interchangeably with the term "third-party administrator" or "TPA." Plan administrators are independent organizations who process all types of benefits or insurance matters. Since ESOPs are a type of benefit, you may be tempted to utilize your company's 401(k) provider as your ESOP administrator for convenience's sake. While it may be efficient to have the same administrator for all retirement plans, be sure that your plan administrator has plenty of experience with leveraged ESOPs. If not, it would be best to choose a separate ESOP administrator.

detail the ESOP share price as well as the value of the individual participants' ESOP shares at the close of the company's plan year. Most companies try to deliver statements to participants as close to their plan year-end as possible. The participant statement will have the stock price for the most recent plan year-end, and the closer the statement is issued to year-end, the easier it will be for participants to correlate the company's performance with the value of their shares. In comparison, if a significant amount of time passes before the statements are issued, and if, for example, the performance of the company changes during that period, it can be difficult for participants to understand why that change is not reflected in their account balance.

Notably, since the plan administrator cannot issue the annual participant statements until a share price is set by the ESOP Trustee, the plan administrator's job relies on completion of the annual ESOP valuation. Once the annual valuation is complete, the company or the Trustee will

PRAIRIE Pointer

provide the per-share stock value to the plan administrator, who then uses the per-share price to determine the value of each participant's account. From there, participant statements are generated and sent to the participants. Depending on the needs of plan participants, the company can request that their plan administrator prepare participant statements in multiple languages.

Once the participants have received their statements, the management team should meet with the participants to explain the statements since it is important to ensure that participants fully understand them. Distribution of annual participant statements also provides management with a great opportunity to discuss the state of the business with the employee-owners and to explain how the company's value drivers are reflected in the ESOP share price. In our experience, plan administrators have also started to become more involved in the explanation of statements to participants.

Typically, someone from the management team – usually the CFO – is the primary point of contact with the plan administrator. However, it is a best practice to have open communication between the plan administrator and the Trustee as well as the rest of the ESOP team so that new ideas or knowledge can be shared easily and at any point in time.

Besides preparing the annual participation statements, the plan administrator has several other responsibilities. For example, the plan administrator provides participants with access to their account information throughout the year. Also, plan administrators get involved when there is a former employee with a vested account balance that cannot be found or when a determination needs to be made as to how a participant's account balance should be split pursuant to issuance of a qualified domestic relations order resulting from the participant's divorce.

Each year, the plan administrator also performs certain regulatory tests. In addition, if the company's CFO wishes, the administrator can prepare reports required by federal agencies, such as IRS Forms 5500 and 1099-R. For their clients with 100 or more participants, the plan administrator may also recommend an outside firm that can conduct the ESOP audit that is required to be done on an annual basis.

In our experience, the best plan administrators also offer consultation services to the ESOP company. These services can include the following: discussions about any unintended consequences resulting from the plan design and how to remedy them; conversations about topics such as repurchase obligation and the plan's long-term sustainability; and monitoring how any cash in the plan is invested.

With regard to selecting a plan administrator, this often happens during the ESOP transaction, although it may also happen immediately after the transaction takes place. In addition, if a company is not satisfied with the service they are receiving from their current plan administrator, the company may want to seek out a new plan administrator. Regardless of the situation, the plan administrator is selected by the Board or, possibly, the ESOP Administration Committee, if one exists. When searching for a plan administrator, it is imperative to find one that is reputable and works on a significant number of ESOP administration projects each year.

In our experience, the best place to start the process of finding a plan administrator is to get several referrals from the company's legal and/or financial advisors. Then, the company can create a request for proposal (RFP) to be sent to prospective administration firms.

Once the company reviews the RFPs submitted by prospective plan administration firms, they should conduct interviews with the firms before making a final decision. When talking to potential plan administrators, focus the information gathering on their experience and how they approach the challenges they face with other clients. In addition, ask what to expect in the short-term as well as the long-term regarding how the ESOP is administered. It is also important to find out how quickly the administrator can finalize participant statements once they receive the ESOP share price. Specifically, ask what they will need in advance from the company and whether they have any strategies to shorten the timeline for statement issuance.

Finally, we do not recommend the internal administration of an ESOP. While it may not seem that difficult to administer the plan internally by, for example, using a spreadsheet system, in our experience, companies that administer the ESOP in-house can encounter major problems at some point in the future. If one mistake is made, it can affect many aspects of the plan – sometimes, even going back several years or more! Because of that, we feel that it is best to give that responsibility to a third-party plan administrator.

CHAPTER 5

The Management Team

TYPICALLY, a company's senior management team consists of a CEO, Chief Operating Officer (COO), CFO, and oftentimes, a Human Resources Director.

Prior to implementation of the ESOP, the seller was most likely part of the senior management team, oftentimes the CEO. Although it is common for the seller to continue to work for the company following implementation of the ESOP, and while some sellers continue in the same role, in other cases, the seller's job title and duties change – sometimes significantly. In addition, once the ESOP is put in place, the seller may be required to sign an employment contract that outlines details such as his/her new role, how long he/she will work for the company, and how he/she will be compensated, including what benefits and perks will be paid for by the company going forward.

PRAIRIE
Pointer

In our experience, in addition to a strong management team, an ESOP company needs to maintain a good operating model. Further, the value drivers of the operating model need to be communicated to the employees in order to ensure the long-term success of the ESOP. Frequent communication is necessary to see the operational and cultural benefits of the ESOP.

At the same time, the seller may choose to stop working for the company on a day-to-day basis but may be elected to the Board.

Further, although it is rare, in some cases, the senior management team that is in place at the time the ESOP is implemented will take over from the seller, and the seller will leave the company entirely. However, it is worth noting that whenever a seller who either founded the business or has owned the business for a long time remains involved in the business, there is a benefit to the company; the seller's knowledge and experience is retained and is readily accessible by the senior management team as well as the Board.

Although the founder may remain with the company after the ESOP is implemented, at some point, the next generation will need to take over and prove that the business is valuable and sustainable without the founder. This transition period can be a risky time for a business. Ultimately, however, a business that transitions away from the founder and proves that it will continue on is a powerful testament to the founder's legacy.

Regardless, in large part, the senior management team's duties remain the same both pre- and post-ESOP implementation. For example, the management team will continue to direct the day-to-day operations of the company, hire and fire employees, and establish compensation levels. Additionally, the management team will continue to execute company strategy and foster the company's culture.

Notably, an important new responsibility the senior management team will need to assume is that of champion of the ESOP. It is especially important for the CEO to be committed to the success of the ESOP and to communicate this commitment to the ESOP participants. As part of this responsibility, it is key for the management team to discuss with the ESOP participants the link between the value drivers of the business (which are discussed further in Chapter 8) and the performance of the ESOP over time. In other words, when teaching employees about the ESOP, it is critical

PRAIRIE
Pointer

If a loan was utilized to finance the ESOP, senior management should keep in mind the importance of consistent communication with the bank regarding the loan's financial covenants. If one or more of the covenants will not be satisfied in any given quarter, the senior management team needs to contact the banker in advance to advise of this fact and to provide a plan outlining how the company will remedy the situation. Bankers will often make an accommodation for a period of time if this type of communication happens. However, if the senior management team does not address a missed covenant, the bank may tighten up the loan agreement, increase the interest rate, or charge a fee. Just remember – bankers hate surprises!

to demonstrate the correlation between company performance, individual performance, and stock value. As part of this process, the CEO will want to lead the effort to establish the company's ESOP Communications Committee as an internal advocacy group and support all of its efforts in educational initiatives. In our experience, when the CEO and senior management team make this type of commitment, the ESOP has a better chance of long-term success.

Additionally, if at any point a new CEO is hired by the company, it is vital to educate the new CEO on the importance of the ESOP so that the new CEO becomes committed to the ESOP's success.

CHAPTER 6

The ESOP Trustee

Section 1 – The ESOP Trustee Overview

Once an ESOP is implemented, the Trustee becomes the fiduciary of the ESOP trust. As a result, the Trustee is essentially responsible for oversight of the ESOP.

Notably, ERISA indicates that Trustees are fiduciaries of the ESOP. In fulfilling their role as a fiduciary, ERISA requires the Trustee to act solely in the interest of ESOP participants and beneficiaries, protect the ESOP's assets, defray reasonable expenses of administering the ESOP, and diversify the investments of the ESOP in an effort to minimize the risk of large losses. Additionally, ERISA requires the Trustee to exercise the same "care, skill, prudence, and diligence under the circumstances then prevailing that a prudent [person] acting in a like capacity and familiar with such matters would use…" If the Trustee fails to satisfy ERISA's fiduciary requirements, they can be held personally liable for their actions – or lack thereof.

In addition to the duties outlined in ERISA, the Trustee has a number of specific ongoing responsibilities which are outlined in the ESOP's trust document (this is frequently, although not always, a separate document from the plan document). Some of the main responsibilities of the Trustee are to:

- Vote the shares of the ESOP to elect the Board
- Hire an experienced, independent appraiser to conduct an annual valuation of the ESOP stock and, based on the valuation, set the stock price
- Manage the assets in the ESOP trust, including issuing checks to eligible participants
- Ensure that the plan is administered properly
- Verify that corporate assets are not used irresponsibly (in conjunction with senior management and the Board)
- Oversee the accounting relating to the ESOP trust, especially if the ESOP has over 100 participants and requires an annual plan audit
- Consider attending one or more board meetings each year
- Thoroughly document all actions

With regard to any voting actions, there are some important distinctions of which to be aware. In the case of a proposed sale of the company, the Trustee is tasked with voting the shares of the ESOP when there is a potential stock sale; however, voting rights are usually required to be passed through to ESOP participants in certain situations such as a merger or consolidation, recapitalization, reclassification, liquidation, dissolution, or a sale of substantially all of the assets of the corporation. When a pass-through vote is required, the participants must be provided with appropriate information on the issue(s) before the vote as well as sufficient time to cast an informed vote, which is typically 20 to 25 business days, depending on jurisdictional requirements. Upon receipt of the results of the pass-through vote, the Trustee will vote the stock on behalf of the participants, based on what the Trustee determines is in the participants' best interest. This means that the Trustee could agree with the results of the pass-through vote but may also choose to vote against the participants' wishes if the Trustee feels that he/she is legally compelled to do so.

Moreover, it is important to note that once the ESOP is put in place, the company can continue to utilize the independent Trustee or fiduciary that was involved with the ESOP transaction, or alternatively, the company can choose a different Trustee.

In terms of selecting a Trustee, the Board is charged with making this choice. While some boards have an ESOP Administration Committee that is responsible for picking the Trustee, others do not, in which case the choice is made by the entire Board.

Regardless, the Board has several options for a Trustee: an independent bank or trust company chartered under state or federal law which provides professional trustee services; a fiduciary firm that provides professional trustee services (usually on an individual basis); or an internal Trustee.

PRAIRIE
Pointer

While a Trustee vote is required in some matters, in others, the company is simply required to give the Trustee notice of a proposed action. So, for example, if a mid-sized company decides to make a material acquisition of a company, the Trustee should be given notice so that they have the opportunity to ensure the deal will not adversely impact the participants. Indeed, in some cases, the Trustee may seek an opinion from a valuation firm regarding the impact of the acquisition. If there is a concern about the transaction, although the Trustee cannot vote to stop the deal, they can tell the company about the reason for their apprehension in the hopes of convincing the company to rethink the proposal.

If the Board plans to use an independent Trustee, several considerations come into play when deciding between a Trustee from a trust company and one from a fiduciary firm, including the following:

- *Cost* – Typically, the fees charged by the larger trust companies are higher than those charged by a fiduciary firm.

- *Risk* – Generally, the larger trust companies have more liability insurance than a fiduciary firm. So, for example, from a balance sheet perspective, if an interested party sues the Trustee, there are usually more resources behind a larger trust company than there would be with a fiduciary firm.

- *Resources* – With a larger trust company, there is generally a bigger team, including a relationship manager who will work with you directly, as well as a committee that will review and vote upon the acceptance of the ESOP's annual valuation. In comparison, fiduciary firms are typically smaller, consisting of a few people.

- *Business Impact* – A larger trust company usually operates on a committee basis, which may make it slower to act on business decisions, as the entire committee must find a time that everyone can meet to make a collective, informed decision. A smaller firm, especially an individual trustee, may expedite any potential decision rather than waiting for a larger, usually slower, institutional trustee committee.

In our experience, when choosing an independent Trustee, the boards of larger companies tend to gravitate toward trust companies, whereas boards at smaller companies often choose fiduciary firms. Ultimately, however, the Board needs to determine whether the services to be provided, the fees to be charged by the Trustee, and the business relationship they are considering fits with the needs of the company.

PRAIRIE Pointer

Notably, while a growing number of companies use a trust company or fiduciary firm, many choose to continue using an internal Trustee. An internal Trustee's interests are usually aligned with those of the participants since they are likely participants in the ESOP themselves. As a result, internal Trustees are typically very motivated to ensure that the ESOP does as well as it can. In addition, internal Trustees usually have a strong understanding of the business and have the ability to make decisions that are not only in the best interest of the ESOP but that are consistent with the company's values and long-term goals. In light of these factors, we see many companies show interest in the possibility of internal Trustees once the ESOP transaction is complete.

There are, however, a few potential negatives related to choosing an internal Trustee. One of the biggest concerns is the fact that the internal Trustee is subject to personal risk since they can be held personally liable for a breach of their fiduciary

Although there is no law prohibiting it, we do not recommend that the selling shareholder(s) serve as the internal Trustee post-transaction. There is significant potential for a conflict of interest to arise if the selling shareholder(s) serves as the internal Trustee because the selling shareholder is usually a large creditor by virtue of a seller note, whereas the internal Trustee is the representative of the equity holders. Therefore, it is a best practice to avoid this entirely. We recommend that the company retains the transactional Trustee until such time as the potential for a DOL or IRS review has expired.

duties. Although the Board should obtain liability insurance for the internal Trustee, some potential candidates for internal Trustees may be reluctant to serve in light of the risk of personal liability.

Additionally, if an internal Trustee fails to receive continuing education about ESOPs, they may be putting themselves at fiduciary risk. There are plenty of quality, cost-effective continuing education offerings through classes such as those that are put on by the NCEO, The ESOP Association (TEA), the Employee-Owned S Corporations of America (ESCA), and others. This will increase the likelihood that the internal Trustee is as well-informed as possible about changes in case law or actions by the DOL that impact ESOPs.

Further, while an internal Trustee's interests may be well-aligned with those of the other participants and the company, sometimes a conflict can develop. For example, if a member of the Board serves as the internal Trustee, at some point, an issue may arise which causes a conflict of interest for the individual in their role as Trustee. In our experience, one of the most common conflicts arises with an internal Trustee who is at or nearing retirement; at that point in the Trustee's life, the ESOP stock price very directly affects their retirement payout from the ESOP, and that may have a bearing on their work as a Trustee. This conflict could be heightened if said employee is a member of the management team that has input over the annual valuation. In addition, providing synthetic equity compensation to parties who might also be a Trustee is a direct conflict of interest.

No matter the type of conflict of interest, a Trustee may elect to seek outside fiduciary guidance to mitigate any personal risk.

Despite possible complications, some companies do choose to utilize an internal Trustee, and often, more than one. If a company chooses this option, we recommend that there is an odd number of internal Trustees so as to avoid a tie on any necessary votes.

In addition, we recommend that a company has no more than three Trustees; having a larger group can become unwieldy, and it can be difficult to find more than three qualified, knowledgeable people to serve as an internal Trustee.

Regardless of whether the company chooses a trust company, fiduciary firm, or an internal individual/group to serve as Trustee, in all of these cases, the Trustee can be fired by the Board. In our experience, common reasons for removal of a Trustee include cost and/or perceived lack of service.

Before the Trustee can be fired, the trustee document (which is found inside the ESOP trust document) usually requires the Trustee to agree to a successor. The trustee document may also contain a notice provision for the Trustee in terms of when the termination can take place. For example, the trustee document may require a 60-day notice before termination. In other cases, the document may indicate that the Trustee cannot be fired within the 30-day period before the end of the plan year. Therefore, if a Board is considering a change in the Trustee, it is important to refer back to the trustee document because it may contain a process outlining how the termination of a Trustee needs to occur.

Section 2 – ESOP Valuation

In order to comply with relevant ERISA and IRS requirements, companies must report the fair market value of privately-held securities within ESOP trusts to the IRS on an annual basis. It is important for the Trustee to select a qualified, independent appraiser to perform the fair market valuation of the stock held in the ESOP trust. Once the independent valuation firm completes the analysis, the Trustee will review the valuation opinion and use that information to set the per-share value of the ESOP stock each year.

Notably, the Trustee has no obligation to share the annual valuation report with the Board unless the Trustee is directed to do so by the ESOP Administration Committee. That said, the Trustee is required to communicate the final per-share price to the Board and the ESOP's plan administrator. The per-share price is also generally communicated to someone within the company's management, such as the CEO or CFO.

An ESOP valuation is different than a valuation for a non-ESOP company. Some considerations that come into play with an ESOP valuation, which may not be an issue with the valuation of a non-ESOP company, include:

- *Synthetic equity* – The impact on the ESOP valuation of SARs, warrants, and other equity-like claims on cash flow

- *ESOP benefit levels* – Participant share allocation "math" and impacts on employee benefit levels

- *ESOP repurchase obligation* – This obligation is a contingent liability of the company that is not reported on the balance sheet but represents the cash obligation of the company to repurchase shares from the ESOP (see Chapter 4, Section 2, for further detail regarding repurchase obligation)

- *Tax treatment* – Many 100% ESOP-owned companies pay little to no income tax because they have elected S-corp status, but the valuation will most likely reflect an imputed C corporation tax rate for the purpose of determining fair market value

- *ESOP internal loan* – How the loan between the company and the ESOP is treated within the valuation

The annual ESOP valuation process is an important part of corporate planning and communication. During the course of the valuation process, the Board and company management will begin to see the interrelatedness of the ESOP stock price; funding

PRAIRIE Pointer

the ESOP; managing benefit levels; repurchase obligation; and communicating the value to participants each year.

Typically, the annual stock valuation begins shortly after a draft of the internally reported year-end results are known. Once the internal year-end results are available, the valuation firm may then conduct its annual due diligence meeting with the company's management and the ESOP Trustee, during which time the valuation firm will ask for information to get an understanding of such factors as the company's core business operations, business model, recent financial performance, competitive position, customer relationships, market conditions, and general business outlook, to name a few.

During due diligence, the valuation firm typically makes a request for items such as the company's organizational chart; historical financial statements; forward-looking budget/projections; information on major customers and revenue per customer; and a list of the company's main competitors. The valuation firm will also likely ask whether the company is involved

Some of the best ESOP-owned companies host an "Annual ESOP Summit" with the company's management and ESOP-related service providers (ESOP Trustee, valuation firm, plan administrator, the company's ESOP counsel, and sometimes the audit firm) to plan for the annual valuation process. An ESOP Summit can also be helpful when contemplating longer-term issues related to ESOP sustainability.

in litigation of any sort, whether the company has received any acquisition offers, and whether any important company agreements have been signed since the ESOP was implemented (or since the last valuation was completed).

When determining the per-share stock value, the valuation firm will look at a point-in-time value (usually the value as of the current plan year-end). The ESOP company should be prepared to discuss with the Trustee and the valuation firm where the company has been and where it is going, similar to the manner in which the company communicates with their banker. Specifically, the company should provide a thorough explanation of current-year results, along with an intermediate-term forecast and support for the forecast inputs. It is best for the company to fully develop its forecast in advance of its meeting with the Trustee's valuation advisor. The forecast should "mesh" with the strategic plan and industry dynamics. Ideally, a five-year forecast that is defensible and is developed by parties with a strong knowledge base is best, as it helps the valuation firm and Trustee understand the company better. This should include strategic insights into the business and its value drivers.

In addition, it may be helpful for management to discuss potential paths that could affect the company's future value trajectory with the Trustee and valuation firm, as many actions taken in the near-term can have long-lasting effects on the ESOP share price. These items, such as how the repurchase obligation is factored into the valuation, the way the company intends to fund and manage its repurchase obligation, etc., should be understood by the Board so that it can best optimize that trajectory going forward.

It is also important for the company to understand what a typical annual ESOP valuation timeline looks like (although the timeline can certainly vary from company to company) and what all of the requirements contained on the timeline – of which there are many – entail. For example, once due diligence is complete, the valuation firm will analyze the information collected and will typically wait for a draft of the financial statements from the firm's certified public accountant (CPA) before creating its draft valuation report for Trustee review. Generally, an ESOP valuation can be concluded with the issuance of the draft audit (or reviewed) financial statements. At the same time, the company's outside CPA firm will need the final ESOP valuation to conclude its work since it will need the ESOP stock price for some of the financial line items. It is extremely important to coordinate the timing of deliverables and communication between the ESOP valuation firm, Trustee, and CPA firm due to the circular nature of these requirements.

A typical annual ESOP valuation timeline for a company with a December 31 year-end may look like this:

JANUARY/FEBRUARY	Company completes internal financial statements and five-year financial forecast
FEBRUARY/MARCH	Draft valuation completed by ESOP valuation firm
MARCH/APRIL	Complete valuation/financial audit/file annual tax forms
APRIL/MAY/JUNE	Complete and distribute participant statements
OCTOBER 15	Form 5500 due to IRS (Technically, the due date is July 15th, but the IRS allows companies to file a three-month extension.)

It is important to note that companies often see dramatic annual increases in equity value and price per-share in the early stages of the ESOP. Often, post-closing, the share price is low, and frequently, the share value benefits from a combination of deleveraging and improving corporate performance after the ESOP is implemented. (Deleveraging is typically accelerated by an advantageous tax structure.) Because of the typical increase in value and price per-share, it is also common to see dramatic annual increases in the participant benefit represented by the ESOP. The participant's

PRAIRIE Pointer

Distribution of annual participant statements provides a great opportunity to communicate with the employee-owners on the state of the business. The closer statement distribution occurs relative to the company's year-end, the more meaningful it will be to employees since events occurring between the valuation date and the date the statements are delivered may not be reflected in the year-end stock price.

aggregate benefit is a reflection of the growing share price as well as the increasing number of shares that are allocated during this time. Communicating this increase in the value trajectory to the employees is a way to get them excited about the ESOP and the company in general, as well as to understand value drivers and what they can do to help boost the ESOP share price.

In light of these and other factors that are unique to ESOP companies, when obtaining a valuation, the Trustee should select an independent valuation firm that has education, credentials, and expertise in valuing ESOPs and that can clearly relay why share prices may fluctuate.

Section 3 – ESOP Legal Counsel

After the ESOP is implemented, legal assistance from an attorney who specializes in ESOP-related matters may be required in a limited number of cases. These include any changes to ERISA or other laws that require the plan document(s) to be amended; the company's desire to amend the plan document in some way; or the company's need to seek guidance as to the application or meaning of the plan document. Regardless, the Trustee must be involved in the discussion and analysis of any changes to the plan.

Additionally, if the company receives a notice from the DOL indicating that the ESOP will be audited, that an investigation will take place, or that the DOL has filed a lawsuit related to the ESOP, the first thing to remember is not to panic! In this case, the Trustee, the Trustee's counsel, and corporate counsel will form a team that will advise the company on the DOL investigation.

Finally, looking longer-term, the company will need assistance from ESOP legal counsel if the company makes an acquisition and wants to incorporate the new employees into the plan; in the case of a proposed sale of the company; when evaluating strategic changes to the ESOP in the face of repurchase obligation projections; or if the ESOP is terminated.

CHAPTER 7

ESOP Communications Committee

AN ESOP Communications Committee is an internal advocacy and education group within an ESOP company. The committee's mission is to educate employees about the ESOP and build a sense of camaraderie and an ownership culture among employees.

While not all ESOP companies have a Communications Committee, the concept is growing in popularity as companies realize the vital importance of communicating with employees in a variety of ways regarding all aspects of the ESOP. In our experience, employees tend to be more receptive to information coming from a group of well-respected peers as opposed to information coming solely from management. The formation of an ESOP Communications Committee enables communication regarding the ESOP to be relayed in an easily accessible manner from a group of peers.

As such, the ESOP Communications Committee seems to work best when composed of eight to 12 respected, non-management individuals within the company who will be well-received by their fellow employees. The manner of members' appointments to the Committee varies widely, depending on the company. Committee members can be selected by management, elected by all employees, or simply volunteer for the position. Sometimes, a representative from Human Resources may be involved since education about the ESOP is an important part of new employees' onboarding process. Regardless, committee members should rotate periodically. Further, when forming an ESOP Communications Committee, the company should keep in mind different demographics within their company that should be represented on the Committee. The company may want to aim for diversity in geography, language, job titles, and responsibilities.

As with all professional committees, your company's ESOP Communications Committee should meet on a regular basis, keep accurate and thorough minutes of the meetings, and keep management informed of the content discussed. Actively communicating with company management assures that the Committee is relaying a message consistent with firm initiatives. In addition, all Committee members should be enrolled in the NCEO, TEA, ESCA, and any local or regional chapters of those associations. These groups are vital resources when the Committee is initially formed, as there may be a need to increase the knowledge base of people wishing to serve on the Committee. Moreover, once the Committee is formed, members can look to these organizations for ideas and content to help them educate and excite employees about the ESOP.

Educating employees about the ESOP is one of the major purposes of the ESOP Communications Committee. This can entail teaching new employees on ESOP basics; giving refresher courses on ESOPs for all employees; assisting the management team in business literacy initiatives; and reinforcing the concept that company performance – and therefore individual and team performance – affects stock value. Committee members may want to promote the concepts of business literacy and value drivers at quarterly

PRAIRIE Pointer

financial meetings by either sponsoring the meeting conducted by the CFO or by delivering the information themselves. In addition, the concept of company performance affecting stock value can be reinforced by Committee members at the annual meeting where participant statements are handed out and discussed. Further, Committee members need to be prepared to communicate in both good times and bad. As stock value increases sharply in the first several years after the ESOP is put in place, Committee members should be involved in the education process about those values eventually tapering off. In addition, in potential "down" years, Committee members, along with the management team, should be communicating along the way so that all employee-owners are well-versed in how company performance directly impacts stock value.

Another purpose of the ESOP Communications Committee is to build a sense of ownership culture within the company. Oftentimes, one of the reasons that the company implemented an ESOP in the first place is a commitment

Communication challenges can abound at ESOP companies with many geographic locations. Some of Prairie's clients have over 100 locations! In those cases, the ESOP Communications Committee should be composed of individuals representing each region or group of locations in order to get representation and buy-in from different regions of the company. Therefore, the Committee can remain in the easily managed eight to 12 member range (though it can be slightly larger as appropriate) but can still represent a variety of employees, projects, and regions.

to sustaining the company's culture. The ESOP Communications Committee's responsibility is to promote that culture while infusing it with new energy surrounding the ESOP. Some of the ways the Committee can promote an ownership culture include the creation and delivery of newsletters or other publications about employees, teams, projects, and events within the company; creating fun, interactive activities for Employee Ownership Month each October; giving meaningful awards to individuals or groups that embody a sense of ownership culture; and organizing exciting and team-building company-wide events to promote camaraderie. It can be helpful for Committee members to attend NCEO, TEA, and ESCA conferences in order to gather ideas for these initiatives.

When supporting the formation of your ESOP Communications Committee, it is imperative to find energetic, well-respected employees who are committed to the ESOP and utilize all of the resources available through the aforementioned groups and associations.

PART 3

What Are We Missing?

CHAPTER 8

Driving Value:
How Personal Finance Literacy, Business Literacy, and Value Drivers Are Interrelated

VALUE drivers are the factors that help create profitability, reduce risk, and promote a company's growth. It is important that all ESOP participants are aware of the company's specific value drivers so that they understand how they can personally go about helping to increase the company's value, which may, in turn, increase the value of the ESOP stock.

However, in our experience, many ESOP participants are not familiar with general business concepts, which can be a major hurdle for an ESOP company; if the participants do not understand basic business or financial terminology and concepts, it is much more likely they will not understand a company's value drivers and how they contribute to the overall growth of the company.

We believe that, in large part, this problem stems from the fact that many people do not have a strong understanding of their own personal finances – let alone a company's finances! Added to that, your employees may be afraid to ask questions about what a business term means because they are embarrassed to admit that they do not understand the meaning and application of the concepts. As a result, employees may forego asking a question about business terminology or value drivers because they are afraid of looking foolish in front of co-workers and management.

However, in our view, if ESOP participants are given the tools to better understand their own personal finances, they will be able to transfer that knowledge and apply it to business concepts. Once they understand broad business concepts, participants will be more likely to understand their specific company's value drivers.

In order to make certain that all participants are knowledgeable about and able to contribute to the growth of the company, clear and frequent communication is vital – not only when initially rolling out the ESOP but also throughout the duration of the ESOP. For instance, quarterly meetings to discuss the company's performance, ongoing employee education, and meetings about ESOP participation statements are all opportunities for the management team to communicate with participants and explain concepts relating to both personal and business finance. Ultimately, the goal is for the ESOP company to see the business grow as more employees become knowledgeable about how personal and business finance work and what they themselves can do to help positively impact the company's value drivers.

Personal Finance Literacy

As mentioned previously, ESOP participants may not be able to fully comprehend what drives the business unless they have a strong understanding of their own finances. An ESOP company can help participants increase their knowledge by educating employees

PRAIRIE Pointer

about personal finance. This will help participants understand their own personal balance sheet and income statement so that they can correlate those concepts with how the business works.

Notably, according to a variety of studies, a large percentage of workers in the U.S. suffer from significant financial stress. In fact, many people do not have enough money in their savings accounts to cover an emergency expense of several hundred dollars. Many workers also worry about their level of debt, saving for retirement, saving for children's education, the cost of day-to-day living expenses, and paying for medical expenses, which results in a significant level of distress. These concerns can affect the ESOP company in two main ways: participants who are stressed financially may have difficulty performing at their highest level, and employees who do not understand their own personal finances will not be able to understand the business's finances well enough to help drive the revenue and profitability of the business and increase the ESOP share price.

Additionally, employees who experience significant financial stress often incur financial costs for their company, in the forms of frequent absenteeism and tardiness, increased healthcare claims,

> If a company wants to make the ESOP work, enhance the company's value, and support its culture, it is imperative that the CEO has a commitment to that mission. The CEO is the driving force in ensuring that the value drivers which are identified and prioritized by the Board are communicated to the ESOP participants and that ESOP participants are fully able to understand how their job performance can impact the value drivers.

turnover, and delayed retirement. Further, employees who are stressed tend to lose focus more easily, thereby costing the company in quality or timeliness of projects completed.

Therefore, we recommend that ESOP companies seriously consider implementing a personal finance literacy program as part of participants' ongoing ESOP education. These types of programs can teach your employees about basic financial concepts. In addition, they may include features such as anonymous personal financial wellness assessments; financial coaching; and suggestions on spending, saving, borrowing, and budget planning. Implementing such a program – many of which are offered through e-learning modules – can help participants in many ways, such as decreasing employee stress levels and destigmatizing the fact that employees may have a lack of knowledge about financial issues. In turn, this may help to prevent or mitigate any expenses the company might incur as a result of employees' financial stress and allow employees to better understand the business.

There are numerous resources and programs that can help ESOP companies with personal finance education. ESOP companies who wish to increase participants' personal finance literacy should look into resources such as the following:

- National Center for Employee Ownership at www.nceo.org
- The ESOP Association at www.esopassociation.org
- Personal Finance Employee Education Fund at www.pfeef.org
- National Financial Educators Council at www.financialeducatorscouncil.org

In addition, each year, accounting firm PricewaterhouseCoopers (PwC) issues its latest findings on personal financial wellness based on its annual Employee Financial Wellness Survey, which is reflective of the financial status of adults in the U.S. who are employed full-time. Survey results include a list of the top financial concerns of survey respondents as well as respondents' ideas about what would help them reach their financial goals. In addition, PwC's survey analysis outlines larger trends in the world of financial wellness, such as issues impacting the overall economy, along with trends occurring within companies in the U.S., which may affect employee financial stress levels. All of the information provided by the survey results and analysis can give leadership within any ESOP company more insight into personal finance literacy statistics and trends. The current year's survey is available at www.pwc.com/us/en/industries/private-company-services/library/financial-well-being-retirement-survey.

Further, most 401(k) providers offer personal finance literacy programs that include e-learning modules, and there are also many independent companies who run personal finance literacy and financial wellness programs. Courses may include personal financial wellness assessments, individualized tutorials, curated articles, and more. In addition, ESOP companies should contact their financial advisors for specific advice and guidance as to what type of program would be best for the company.

Regardless of which program the company implements, at a very basic level, it is important for ESOP participants to become familiar with the following terms and be able to apply them to their own financial situation:

PERSONAL BALANCE SHEET	PERSONAL INCOME STATEMENT
• Assets (house, savings, etc.) • Liabilities (mortgage, car loan) • Net Worth	• Budget • Cash Flow

A good way to introduce the concept of a balance sheet is by use of an example that relates to many participants' lives. Most participants will understand that if they purchase a $200,000 home with a $150,000 mortgage, they have $50,000 equity in the home. As they pay off the mortgage over time, they build more equity, with the ultimate goal being to pay off the mortgage so that 100% of the value of the home is theirs. This example shows how a balance sheet works: equity is determined by subtracting the mortgage balance from the home's value. Using the personal residence example can help participants make an intuitive connection to the changing value of the business over time.

During this discussion, simple questions can emerge: What happens to the home equity value if the home's price increases by 5%? What happens to equity value over time if the employee takes out a second mortgage and puts an addition onto the home? A baseline understanding of these concepts can go a long way toward helping employees appreciate how their actions to add value can translate to additions to the company's value.

In our experience, management teams sometimes assume that employees have this basic level of knowledge about personal finance, especially in companies with employees that have a higher-than-average education level. However, that is not always the case. We believe that it is imperative for the management team to ensure this baseline knowledge is attained by employees across the board.

Business Literacy

Once ESOP participants are knowledgeable about personal finance, they will be better able to understand basic business concepts. Business literacy is defined as understanding basic business terminology as well as the terminology that is specific to your individual business.

Participants who want to try to help improve the income of the business need to learn how to "speak" business. In general, some basic terminology that all participants should understand and be able to apply to the company include the following:

COMPANY BALANCE SHEET	COMPANY INCOME STATEMENT
• Assets • Liabilities • Net Worth (Equity)	• Budget • Revenue • Gross Margin • Net Income • Cash Flow

Remember, just as in the case of personal finance, do not assume that all ESOP participants are knowledgeable about this terminology – no matter what education level they have or position they hold within the company. Additionally, participants should not only be able to define these concepts but also understand how they work within the context of your business.

As an example of business terminology and its application, "profitability" is a term with which every participant should be familiar, as it is a value driver for all companies. We have found that, while participants may think they know what profitability means, in reality, many do not. For instance, your employees may confuse the terms "revenue" and "profit." If that is the case, when an ESOP company tells the participants that revenue was $10 million during the prior fiscal year, some participants may conclude that the company had a $10 million profit. It could then be confusing to the participant if the ESOP share price does not increase significantly during that fiscal year. In order to mitigate such confusion, basic business literacy is needed.

One way that an ESOP company can help participants better understand business terminology is by tying it to the knowledge that participants gain as part of the educational opportunities the company provides regarding personal finance. For example, once the participants are able to develop their own personal balance sheet, they will be better equipped to comprehend the company's balance sheet. Further, once the participants put together their own personal income statement – which is, essentially, their household budget – they will have a better understanding of the company's income statement. For instance, if a family makes $100,000 per year, they may spend $25,000 on taxes, leaving $75,000 to pay for food, utilities, car payments, housing expenses, etc. Once those costs are paid, the family may be left with $5,000 for the year, which is the profitability of the household. By making the connection between their own budget and the company's income statement, the participant will more easily see that, even if the company takes in $10 million during the year, they certainly will not keep all $10 million and must instead use that revenue to pay off expenses and taxes. Any money remaining is, of course, the company's profit.

In a similar manner, explaining the amount of equity outlined on the company's balance sheet can be done more easily by using participants' knowledge of how to calculate their own net worth and showing participants how personal net worth is the equivalent of equity on a company's balance sheet. In any case, drawing these types of parallels between personal and business finances can help ESOP participants appreciate how the work they do can impact the value of the company.

With regard to the types of resources an ESOP company can use to teach business literacy, many of the resources listed in the previous section regarding personal finance literacy will also apply in this context, especially the resources found through the NCEO. In addition, one of the more notable programs for business literacy is through The Great Game of Business, which uses the open-book management philosophy. There are other programs that use open-book management that are also effective.

Value Drivers

Once the ESOP participants are confident in their understanding of their personal finances and can apply that knowledge to basic business concepts, they can better understand how to drive the value of the ESOP company. The Board will tell management what value drivers should be communicated to the participants, and it is the management team's responsibility to determine how the value drivers will be relayed.

There are some value drivers over which the company and its employees have little or no control. These are called external value drivers, and they include global issues, economic issues, industry issues, the competitive landscape, investor psychology, the political environment, legislation, taxes, interest rates, and lending conditions. While it is important that the Board and the

Helping Participants Become Familiar With Value Drivers

To better help participants understand the company's value drivers, you may consider using a real-life example.

For instance, imagine that the ESOP company you run manufactures plastic cups. Due to an issue with quality control, some batches of plastic cups develop small cracks, and the cracks are not caught before shipment. One million cups ship to a superstore that receives complaints from customers who discover the cups do not hold water. Customers return the cups to the superstore, and, in turn, the superstore complains to you – the manufacturer – and demands credit for all of the faulty cups they purchased. If the superstore paid five cents for each cup, the ESOP company loses $50,000 in revenue, thereby reducing cash flow and potentially stymying the company's growth. Further, the superstore may have lost faith in the product and may cancel future orders as a result. Alternatively, if the superstore does continue to do business with your company, they may leverage the faulty cup ordeal by demanding to pay 4.5 cents per cup instead of the original five cents – a 10% loss that will decrease profitability.

Using an illustration like this within the context of your own company can help participants understand that they can directly impact the company's value. In this case, quality control was the main issue. What would the issue be in your company's example?

management team are aware of these factors and communicate to the participants any impact external value drivers have on the ESOP share value, we anticipate that senior management will spend less time discussing external value drivers with the ESOP participants than they will discussing internal value drivers.

All participants should be aware of internal value drivers since those are factors that the company can better control (although external value drivers will inevitably affect the internal value drivers for better or worse). Overall, the value drivers that every business should be monitoring and relaying to the employees are revenue, growth, and profitability. Depending on the company and its goals, other important internal value drivers to be discussed with participants may include balance sheet factors, intangible assets, customer diversification, size, capital requirements, litigation, and environmental issues.

Several years ago, during a manufacturing plant tour, an employee at the manufacturing company shared an example with the Prairie team as to how one employee can significantly impact a company's stock value.

The employee made a suggestion that enabled the manufacturing company to improve the flow of materials and save time. He estimated this suggestion yielded an annual savings of $150,000 for the company. In response, the Prairie team told him that, as part of the valuation process, this particular manufacturing company was valued at about six times pre-tax cash flow. Therefore, his idea also created about $1.0 million of new value that he and his coworkers would eventually share as participants in the ESOP because of the resulting increase in the ESOP share price.

Notably, in an ESOP company, the culture is also often a major internal value driver. A positive culture leads to lower turnover and a higher degree of satisfaction with the job. We have found that, if the ESOP company has good values and infuses them into the day-to-day life of the business, participants will want to help grow the business. Keeping the company's "finger" on the pulse of the culture and having open communication about it can help drive the value of the business.

Regardless of value drivers that the company wishes to communicate to the participants, it is crucial that participants have a baseline knowledge of the business terminology that the company uses. If the company has invested the time in making sure that all participants have attained basic business literacy levels, relaying the value drivers should just be a matter of communicating them clearly on a regular basis.

In practice, the ESOP company should have – at a minimum – quarterly meetings to communicate these value drivers, led by the management team. With all of the technological options available, such as online meeting technology, it is easy to connect all locations of a company for these types of meetings, though certainly, at times, it may be appropriate to consider having localized communications at individual locations as well. Further, ESOP companies also need to consider their company's needs regarding the languages in which value drivers will be communicated and/ or the number of presentations that need to be made available if the company has shift workers. Regardless of the structure or locations of the communications, it is key that the message about value drivers be consistent throughout the ESOP company, irrespective of the participants' job title, language, or shift.

CHAPTER 9

Preparing for the Possible Sale of the ESOP Company

THE POSSIBILITY of selling the company is not typically a priority for the senior management team or Board at a company with a newly installed ESOP. Instead, most companies are focused on paying off the debt that was incurred to finance the ESOP. Nevertheless, there are a variety of reasons why – at some point in the future – senior management and the Board may consider the possibility of a sale.

In our experience, if an ESOP-owned company is contemplating a sale of the business, it is not generally because the company is proactively seeking a buyer. Rather, most successful ESOP companies that are considering a sale have received an unsolicited purchase offer from a private equity firm or a competitor in the same or a similar industry.

Still, there may be circumstances that result in an ESOP-owned company affirmatively seeking out a potential buyer. For instance, if the company requires additional capital but is not comfortable with taking on debt, selling the company may become an option.

In any event, because the sale of an ESOP-owned company often results from an unsolicited purchase offer, it is important for the company's senior management and Board to be prepared to respond to this type of offer. In our experience, while it may be tempting to immediately dismiss an unsolicited offer, it would be legally prudent to consider the proposal at the very least. In that regard, some Boards choose to establish a committee to review purchase offers; if no such committee is formed, the full Board will need to formulate a plan to respond. Notably, if a company receives a bona fide purchase offer, the senior management team and the Board should review and consider it, as the offer may unlock significant value for the ESOP participants. Moreover, while the company's management team should treat any offers which are received seriously, there is no specific requirement to inform the Board of an offer unless it is bona fide.

More often than not, if the management team and/or the Board have a negative reaction after considering a bona fide offer, the possibility of a sale will likely end at that point. On the other hand, if they are interested in exploring the possibility of a sale further, the company and the potential buyer usually exchange confidentiality agreements – also known as non-disclosure agreements – and will then customarily share cursory information about their businesses in order to gain a better understanding of each other. This could include, for example, information on the size of each company and what they do. Under *no* circumstances should the company provide a potential buyer a copy of the annual ESOP valuation.

At that point, if the Board and senior management remain interested in moving forward with a possible sale, they should involve the ESOP Trustee in the sale discussions and negotiations. The Board and the Trustee also need to determine if, in order to satisfy their fiduciary responsibilities, a broader sales and marketing process would be advisable.

PRAIRIE Pointer

Ultimately, there may be a number of possible reasons an ESOP company decides to sell – including circumstances that are unique to the company. However, we have found that some of the more common reasons an ESOP-owned company's Board elects to sell include the following:

- *Monetary Benefits* – A sale can result in a significant increase in the value of ESOP shares, especially if the buyer pays a market premium. According to the NCEO, in many sale transactions, participants see their ESOP share value rise in the range of 25% to 100%. Notably, we have found that an ESOP Trustee will generally only agree to sell the company if there is an appropriate premium attached to the previous share price. As a result of a sale, not only does the per-share price for ESOP stock increase, but a sale can also help the company gain liquidity and fund participants' ESOP accounts; in turn, this may help address any difficulties the company is experiencing with its repurchase obligation.

An offer is considered "bona fide" if:

✔ the proposed consideration is nominally adequate;

✔ the other terms of the proposed deal are fair, reasonable, and treat all shareholders equitably; and,

✔ the potential buyer has the financial ability to pay the proposed purchase price.

PRAIRIE Pointer

When initially considering how to respond to an unsolicited offer, the Board may choose to discuss a possible sale directly with the potential buyer. Alternatively, the Board may decide to engage an investment banking firm to help evaluate the company's options with regard to a possible sale. For instance, an investment banker can help the company assess whether the purchase offer is in line with, above, or below market pricing; if the terms of the potential sale can be improved; or if the company would be better off going to market in search of other purchase offers.

Regardless, in order to ensure the integrity of any sale that takes place, it is important for all parties involved to engage independent advisors to safeguard their interests and make certain all required steps occur.

- *Added Capabilities* – If an ESOP company sells to another firm in their industry, they often gain capabilities that they did not have before the sale. For example, the buyer may bring talent and/or an organizational structure that will help bring the company to the next level of success.

- *Market Trends* – If the industry in which the ESOP company operates is experiencing a high degree of volatility, the company may determine it is best to sell in order to protect the company's – and the ESOP's – assets. Further, if there is an industry trend toward consolidation – as a result of which many of the company's competitors are being acquired – a sale may be a good option in that it may allow the seller to remain competitive in the industry.

- *Management Succession Issues* – If the company's senior management team is nearing retirement age and the company lacks strong internal candidates to succeed the existing senior management, the company may decide to sell in order to capitalize on the current performance of the company.

At the same time, there are a number of reasons that an ESOP-owned company's Board may decide against selling, including the following:

- *Loss of Company Culture* – The culture of a successful ESOP-owned company is often unique. There is a risk that, if the business is sold to a new owner, the culture of the two companies will clash and the ESOP company's culture will not be preserved, which can impact the morale of the staff. In our experience, the loss of culture can result in a sale that is not as successful as the parties anticipated.

- *Change in Governance* – When a sale occurs, there will most likely be a new senior management team – or at least part of the team will be new – as well as a new Board. Some ESOP companies are reluctant to sell because of the uncertainty related to how this new group of leaders will act and whether they will be effective and accepted by the employees.

- *Job Loss/Consolidation* – When a sale takes place, there is always a possibility that the buyer may shut down facilities or reduce the number of staff, especially when they have their own. While the ESOP company may be aware of these plans prior to a sale, there is also the chance that the buyer will not disclose their intentions until after the sale is complete – sometimes not until months or more after the deal closes.

- *The Potential for Added Value* – While the pricing of the deal may seem attractive on the surface, some ESOP companies actually have the potential to sell at a higher price and, thus, further enhance the value of the ESOP accounts. ESOP Trustees and ESOP investment bankers are aware of this possibility, and it frequently is a negotiating point that can lead to the company to rejecting the offer.

- *Confidentiality and Closing Risks* – When a company is involved in a sale process, there is a chance that the sale will not be finalized. However, as part of the sale process, the company usually provides the potential buyer access to confidential information about the business. If the deal does not ultimately close and the potential buyer is a competitor, there may be a concern that the potential buyer will use that confidential information to compete more effectively with the company.

Notably, after considering the pros and cons related to a sale, the Board may decide to accept a purchase offer. However, before a sale can be finalized, the Trustee has to vote the ESOP stock either in favor of or against the deal. In addition, depending on the type of sale, the vote may need to be passed through to the ESOP participants.

There are two basic types of sales: a purchase of assets and a purchase of stock. With a purchase of assets, the buyer receives the company's assets and may or may not take on the company's liabilities. In comparison, if the buyer purchases the company's stock, they take on the liabilities as well as the assets.

Although the plan document will have more specific directions, in general, if the buyer proposes a purchase of stock, the Trustee can decide whether or not to move forward without input from the participants. However, if the buyer wishes to purchase the company's assets, the vote is typically required to be passed through to the plan participants who will need to cast a ballot in favor of or against a sale of the company's assets.

In that case, the company will need to provide participants with a descriptive memorandum outlining detailed financial information, what will happen if the sale takes place, when the sale will take place, and how much money participants are expected to receive as a result of the sale. Participants will be given a date by which their vote must be cast. The votes will then be tallied by the plan

PRAIRIE Pointer

administrator or a law firm, and the results will be provided to the Trustee. The possibility of a participant vote should be raised early on because it adds time to the closing schedule that non-ESOP investment bankers and acquirers may not anticipate.

Notably, since the Trustee's ultimate responsibility is to act in the best interest of the ESOP, if the Trustee determines that the outcome of the participants' vote is not actually in the ESOP's best interest, the Trustee can theoretically supersede the participant vote if the Trustee believes it would be a breach of their fiduciary duty to follow the participant's vote. However, this is extremely rare.

If a sale ultimately takes place, in most cases, the ESOP will be terminated. However, before the ESOP can be completely terminated, all participants – including those that are no longer employees of the company – will need to be paid. In our estimation, on average, it takes about two years to conclude the operations of an ESOP, and participants are often not paid

Contingent consideration, payments for non-compete agreements, escrows, and holdbacks are some possible issues which may arise post-closing. These are normal, commercially acceptable deal elements, but they can complicate the distribution of proceeds and, in particular, the proceeds flowing to ESOP participants. Companies should hold a detailed session on these issues with their corporate and ESOP counsel at an early stage. It is quite possible that the structure of the transaction could be adjusted to lessen the impact of these items.

for a year or more after the sale transaction closes. As a result, the Trustee will remain in place until all of the ESOP termination activities are complete.

During that time, the company will be involved in several activities, such as completing the necessary paperwork for the IRS; working with the plan administrator to allocate participant shares; and demonstrating that all participant distributions have been made. If there are participants that cannot be located, the company must also show that it made a good faith effort to find those people.

PART 4

What Might Our Post-Closing Checklist Include?

Post-Closing Transactional Matters

Although this list is not all-inclusive, following is a checklist of some of the pertinent items that may require your attention post-closing, as well as on an ongoing basis.

Matters To Review Shortly After Closing

Soon after the ESOP transaction closes, there are several items that may need your immediate attention, as outlined below.

TASK	DUE DATE	RESPONSIBLE PARTIES

1. Insurance – confirm that policies align with new ESOP structure.
   a. Directors and officers liability insurance policy
   b. Additional ESOP fiduciary coverage for board members
   c. Key person life insurance
	ASAP post-closing (pre-closing if possible)	Board (with help of insurance broker and potentially corporate counsel)

2. Management Incentive Plan (may include annual bonus, Long-Term Incentive Plan, SARs, Phantom Stock, or other form of incentive-based compensation)
   a. Establish Compensation Committee of the board, if desired.
   b. Adopt board resolution authorizing awards.
   c. For stock-based compensation, obtain valuation for post-transaction strike price.
   d. Consider professional compensation study to evaluate proper compensation levels.
   e. Provide copy of signed awards to recipients, auditors, and Trustee.
	ASAP post-closing	Board (with help of corporate counsel and potentially ESOP Trustee and valuation firm)

Matters to Review continued

TASK	DUE DATE	RESPONSIBLE PARTIES
3. Final calculation of closing working capital a. Possible working capital adjustment may result in a cash distribution to sellers or changes to seller notes. b. If changes to seller notes are required, the company may need to notify Trustee and bank of revised seller note amortization schedules.	Usually within 60-90 days following closing	CFO (with possible help of accounting firm and sign off by Trustee and valuation firm)
4. Ensure company stock ledger is up-to-date and in order.	ASAP post-closing	CFO and Board (with possible help from corporate counsel)
5. Ensure receipt of final transaction closing binder.	ASAP post-closing	CFO and Board (with possible help from corporate counsel)
6. S Election filing – Oftentimes, ESOP transactions result in a change in corporate structure and/or tax status. For 100% ESOP-owned companies, it is usually advantageous to make an election to be taxed as an S-corp.	Tax election deadline	CEO (with help of tax advisor and corporate counsel)
7. Ensure that the share certificate is under custody. In the future, should there be any changes in the number of shares outstanding, the certificate must be amended to reflect the change.	ASAP post-closing	CFO or Secretary of the Board, if required by state law

Communication

Ongoing communications regarding the ESOP should be a priority, not only in the ESOP's early days but also over time.

TASK	DUE DATE	RESPONSIBLE PARTIES
1. Make reservations/plans for closing dinner.	ASAP	Chief Marketing Officer
2. Develop initial communications materials for ESOP rollout: a. Create an agenda for employee rollout meetings and any materials to be distributed. b. Create and distribute press release. c. Update website and marketing materials with new company name, if applicable, and employee-owned status. d. Add SPD to internal company website/intranet. e. If desired, establish internal ESOP Communications Committee and enroll member in the NCEO, TEA, and the local ESOP Association chapter. Also, sign up for Prairie Capital Advisors' email list, found at www.prairiecap.com, to receive ESOP-related articles, information regarding webinars that discuss ESOP-related topics, and more. f. Ask ESOP Communications Committee to report to the Board at least once per year on items such as ESOP communication efforts. g. Make arrangements for CEO and CFO to attend ESOP-related roundtable events.	As ready	Chief Marketing Officer and Human Resources Director

Banking

Good communication with your banker is critical to help them understand that the ESOP's impact on your business may be an important part of the financial success of the business going forward. In our experience, it is a good idea to ask your banker for the formatted spreadsheet they use to compile information needed for credit and covenant testing. It can make communications with your banker more efficient.

TASK	DUE DATE	RESPONSIBLE PARTIES
1. Monitor cash, line of credit, and working capital balances in compliance with bank limits.	Daily	CFO
2. Update cash flow coverage models to ensure compliance with cash flow needs and covenant models.	Weekly	CFO
3. Covenant Testing – Monitor coverage levels prior to paying interest on seller notes or making capital expenditures.	Monthly, Quarterly, or Annually, as required by the lender	CFO
4. Complete and certify borrowing base certificate, if applicable.	Monthly	CFO

Corporate Governance

An effective Board is an important factor in an ESOP company's success.

TASK	DUE DATE	RESPONSIBLE PARTIES
1. Identify and nominate directors, including independent directors.	Varies	Board (Trustee will vote on nominees)
2. Enroll board members in corporate governance and fiduciary training.	ASAP following election of new directors	Board
3. Once established, the Board should adopt committee charters and appoint committee members.	ASAP following election of new directors	Board
4. Verify if any IRS/DOL guidelines or revenue rulings or any court decisions impact the company's ESOP.	Once each plan year	Board and ESOP Legal Counsel
5. Corporate Governance/General a. Evaluate Board fees and insurance amounts. b. Set annual calendar for both Board and Committee meetings. c. Consider sending board members to employee ownership conference(s) to supplement their ESOP education.	Ongoing	Board

Reporting and Disclosure Under ERISA

ESOPs have some important deadlines. Although this list may not be comprehensive, you need to be aware of these reporting and disclosure requirements under ERISA and the Internal Revenue Code.

TASK	DUE DATE	RESPONSIBLE PARTIES
1. Distribute SPD to participants.	ASAP/no later than 90 days after closing. After that date, new participants should receive an SPD within 90 days of becoming a participant.	Human Resources Director and CFO
2. Submit the plan document to the IRS requesting Favorable Determination Letter (Form 5300).	ASAP post-closing	CFO and ESOP Counsel
3. File Form 5500 with IRS.	Annually, by the last day of the seventh month after the plan year-end (July 31 for a calendar-year plan). An optional extension is available to the 15th day of the third month after the filing deadline (October 15 for a calendar-year plan). (See www.irs.gov for further details.)	CFO

Reporting and Disclosure continued

TASK	DUE DATE	RESPONSIBLE PARTIES
4. Provide updated summary of Material Modifications to participants.	Each time the plan is materially amended	Human Resources Director, CFO, and ESOP Legal Counsel
5. Provide participants with Summary Annual Report.	Nine months after the end of each plan year	Human Resources Director and CFO
6. Provide participants with annual statements.	At least once each calendar year	Human Resources Director and CFO

Financial Reporting/ESOP Valuation

Each year, there are a number of financial reports to be assembled by ESOP companies.

TASK	DUE DATE	RESPONSIBLE PARTIES
1. Make payment on ESOP internal loan.	Annually, as applicable	CFO
2. Prepare draft of audited financial statements.	First quarter following fiscal year-end	CFO (with audit firm)
3. Develop five-year financial forecast. a. Submit for Board approval. b. Provide to Trustee and bank once approved.	Prior to annual due diligence meeting with Trustee and valuation firm	CFO and Board
4. Schedule and participate in annual due diligence meeting with Trustee and valuation firm.	Usually within five months following the end of each plan year	CEO and CFO
5. Complete ESOP valuation report.	Usually within six months following the end of each plan year	Valuation firm and Trustee

ESOP Administration

The plan administrator is responsible for all record keeping and reporting requirements, as well as the day-to-day operations of an ESOP.

TASK	DUE DATE	RESPONSIBLE PARTIES
1. Purchase ESOP fiduciary bond.	Every year	CFO (with plan administrator)
2. Prepare eligible compensation and employee census data for plan administrator.	Following the end of each plan year	CFO and Human Resources Director
3. Complete annual ESOP administration and accounting/delivery of participant account statements.	Once each plan year	CFO (with plan administrator)
4. Ensure 409(p) testing is completed for every year that the corporation is an S corporation.	Annually as applicable	CFO (with plan administrator)
5. Offer stock diversification option to eligible participants.	Typically does not apply until 10 years after ESOP is implemented	CFO (with plan administrator)
6. Make ESOP distributions to terminated participants.	Once each plan year	CFO (with plan administrator)
7. Conduct annual recalculation of suspense account shares and allocated shares, and prepare new stock certificates for the same.	Following the end of each plan year	CFO (with plan administrator)
8. Obtain a repurchase obligation study.	Usually recommended every three years or as needed	CFO and Board

Conclusion

Hopefully, the information contained in this book has made you feel more comfortable as a leader in a newly-formed ESOP company.

Undoubtedly, throughout the process of implementing the ESOP, you have realized that ensuring the success of an ESOP is a team-based effort. It is important to remember that everyone on your team – from board members to the management team, from Trustee to plan administrator, from employee-owners to your valuation firm and trusted advisors – be part of the ongoing effort to help your company and its ESOP thrive.

Remember, any time you have a question, it is essential to reach out to your trusted advisors for assistance. Prairie Capital Advisors would welcome the opportunity to work with you on any of your valuation, ESOP advisory, and investment banking needs.

Acknowledgements

WRITING A BOOK IS A TEAM EFFORT, AND OUR TEAM IS TRULY LIKE NO OTHER.

Many thanks to Lauren Hajek and Nicole Gombotz for planning, organizing, and executing the writing process from the initial interviews to the final edits. This book would not have come together without their efforts.

Much appreciation goes to Wendy Gugora who did the heavy lifting on the logistics and publishing end.

In addition, we would like to extend our gratitude to Robert Gross for his editing skills and added insights.

Further, many thanks to David Diehl, Rocky Fiore, Richard Shuma, Hillary Hughes, and Christine Myers for being our first readers and providing us with invaluable feedback. We would also like to acknowledge Anthony Dolan for providing his insights on selling ESOP companies. Finally, much appreciation goes to Vincent DiRaddo, Timothy Witt, Macie Dorow, and Nicholas Dolan for assisting with questions along the way.

Further Reading

If you would like to dig deeper on any of the subjects in this book, we recommend you consult the following resources:

- Prairie Capital Advisors at www.prairiecap.com
- National Center for Employee Ownership (NCEO) at www.nceo.org
- The ESOP Association at www.esopassociation.org
- Employee-Owned S Corporations of America (ESCA) at www.esca.us
- Certified EO at www.certifiedeo.com
- The Great Game of Business at www.greatgame.com
- Personal Finance Employee Education Fund (PFEEF) at www.pfeef.org
- National Financial Educators Council at www.financialeducatorscouncil.org

References

Chapter 1 – Rolling Out the ESOP to Participants

NCEO. (2014). *The ESOP communications sourcebook, sixth edition.* Oakland, CA: NCEO.

Chapter 2 – ESOP Stock: Who Gets It? What Happens to It? And, How Do Participants Get Paid?

NCEO. When will I be paid? The ESOP participant's guide to ESOP distribution rules. Retrieved from https://www.nceo.org/articles/esop-participant-distribution-rules

Chapter 3 – The Rights of ESOP Participants

NCEO. The rights of ESOP participants. Retrieved from https://www.nceo.org/articles/rights-esop-participants

Chapter 4 – Board of Directors/Repurchase Obligation & Sustainability/ ESOP Administration Committee/ESOP Plan Administrator

Barry, D. (2017). Preparing for ESOP repurchase obligations. *Pensions & Investments.* Retrieved from https://www.pionline.com/article/20170406/ONLINE/170409961/preparing-for-esop-repurchase-obligations

Coffey, M.A. & Tilley, L.J. (2015). Effective ESOP administrative committees. Corporate Capital Resources. Retrieved from http://www.ccrva.com/wp-content/uploads/2016/07/CCR-NCEO-Effective-ESOP-Committees-November-2015.pdf

Diehl, D. Repurchase obligation studies & the other importance of future share price estimates. Prairie Capital Advisors. Retrieved from http://www.prairiecap.com/Websites/prairiecap/images/Whitepaper_Repurchase_Obligation_Studies.pdf

Matthews, A. (2000). *The ESOP administrator's notebook*. NCEO. Retrieved from https://www.nceo.org/esop-administrators-notebook/c/governing-esops-esop-companies

NCEO. *Duties of the ESOP committee.* Retrieved from https://www.nceo.org/articles/duties-esop-committee

Rosen, C. & Ritterspach, K. (2015). *Sustainable ESOPs.* NCEO. Retrieved from https://www.nceo.org/Sustainable-ESOPs/pub.php/id/744/

Silva, F. *Creating a strategy for a sustainable ESOP company.* Prairie Capital Advisors. Retrieved from http://www.prairiecap.com/Websites/prairiecap/images/Prairie_Sustainable_ESOP_Company.pdf

Chapter 5 – The Management Team

Blenko, M., Garton, E., & Mottura, L. (2014). *Winning operating models that convert strategy to results.* Bain & Company. Retrieved from https://www.bain.com/insights/winning-operating-models-that-convert-strategy-to-results/

Garton, E. (2017). *Is your company actually set up to support your strategy?* Harvard Business Review. Retrieved from https://hbr.org/2017/11/is-your-company-actually-set-up-to-support-your-strategy

Chapter 6 – The ESOP Trustee/ESOP Valuation/ESOP Legal Counsel

Cornell Law School. *29 U.S. Code 1104. Fiduciary duties.* Retrieved from https://www.law.cornell.edu/uscode/text/29/1104

Kalman, Y.I. & Novak, M.A. (2018). *What expenses can we pay from plan assets? A brief review of the legal principles and some common questions.* Drinker Biddle. Retrieved from https://www.drinkerbiddle.com/insights/publications/2018/05/what-expenses-can-we-pay-from-plan-assets

Schechter, C.F. (2018). *What are the "reasonable" expenses that can be paid out from plan assets?* Butterfield Schechter LLP. Retrieved from https://www.bsllp.com/reasonable-expenses-from-plan-assets

Chapter 7 – ESOP Communications Committee

NCEO. (2014). *The ESOP communications sourcebook, sixth edition.* Oakland, CA: NCEO.

References

Chapter 8 – Driving Value: How Personal Finance Literacy, Business Literacy, and Value Drivers Are Interrelated

Bolden-Barrett, V. (2017). 1 in 3 workers say their personal finances are distracting at work. *HR Dive*. Retrieved from https://www.hrdive.com/news/1-in-3-workers-say-their-personal-finances-are-distracting-at-work/444265/

Gerstley, A.F. (2017). What employees' financial unwellness is costing their companies. *Forbes*. Retrieved from https://www.forbes.com/sites/ellevate/2017/09/07/what-employees-financial-unwellness-is-costing-their-companies/#64ccb23b55f9

McGinley, M. & O'Neill, A. (2017). NCEO: Valuation basics. Prairie Capital Advisors.

Miller, S. (2016). Employees' financial issues affect their job performance. Society for Human Resource Management. Retrieved from https://www.shrm.org/resourcesandtools/hr-topics/benefits/pages/employees-financial-issues-affect-their-job-performance.aspx

PwC. (2018). 2018 employee financial wellness survey. Retrieved from https://www.pwc.com/us/en/industries/private-company-services/library/financial-well-being-retirement-survey.html

Chapter 9 – Preparing for the Possible Sale of the ESOP Company

NCEO. (2014). *The ESOP communications sourcebook, sixth edition*. Oakland, CA: NCEO.

Prairie Capital Advisors. Selling an ESOP company. Retrieved from http://www.prairiecap.com/selling-an-esop-company3

About Prairie Capital Advisors, Inc.

PRAIRIE CAPITAL ADVISORS (Prairie) provides investment banking, ESOP advisory, and valuation advisory services to support the growth and ownership transition strategies of middle-market companies. Prairie's advisors help business owners understand, evaluate, and implement ESOPs as well as a wide variety of other ownership transition strategies.

Prairie's mission is to provide each client with independent advice and highly personalized service to help the client meet their objectives and maximize shareholder value.

In addition, Prairie is an employee-owned company. Prairie's ESOP was implemented on January 1, 2012, and it provides qualified employees with 43% ownership of the firm.

About the Authors

KENNETH E. SERWINSKI

Mr. Serwinski co-founded Prairie with Robert Gross in 1996 after the pair of industry veterans recognized that there was a universally underserved need for objective financial advisory consultation for closely-held businesses. Since then, Mr. Serwinski has dedicated his experience to providing closely-held companies with the guidance and expertise needed for some of their most critical business decisions. Today, he continues to develop Prairie's reputation as the most widely-respected firm of its kind, designing and implementing customized ownership transition strategies, including private sales, management buyouts, ESOPs, and more, for businesses nationwide.

Many companies seek out and trust Mr. Serwinski and Prairie for strategic guidance on once-in-a-lifetime business decisions. Whether they require expertise in ownership transition, valuation, capital management, or something else, Mr. Serwinski begins each client relationship not with a pre-fabricated solution, but with the question, "What are you trying to achieve?" He and his team then develop the most appropriate solutions to deliver the best outcomes for the client.

As a lifelong educator and respected industry expert, Mr. Serwinski is widely published on a variety of financial advisory topics and is a frequent speaker around the nation on subjects including valuation, ESOPs, and ownership transition planning. Whether he is across the table from clients or speaking publicly at workshops and seminars, he strives to ensure business owners have the complete, accurate information they need for confident decision making. Mr. Serwinski sits on the board of directors of two businesses – a healthcare solutions provider and a bank. He also is the former Chair of the Advisory Committee on Finance for The ESOP Association in Washington, D.C.

MICHAEL J. McGINLEY

Mr. McGinley specializes in all aspects of ownership transition and financial advisory services to business owners, boards of directors, and trustees, including ESOPs, mergers and acquisitions, capital raising, and the valuation of businesses and business interests for gift and estate tax planning, strategic planning, financial accounting and reporting, buy-sell agreements, and dispute resolution. He currently serves as a member of The ESOP Association's Valuation Advisory Committee.

Mr. McGinley was recognized as a 2017 "40 Under Forty" honoree by the National Association of Certified Valuators and Analysts.

Mr. McGinley provides financial advisory services primarily to middle-market, privately-held businesses in a wide range of industries such as architecture/ engineering/construction, automotive, biotechnology, chemical, consumer goods, distribution, energy, entertainment, financial services (including accounting, banking, and investment management), government contracting, food and restaurant, healthcare and dentistry, technology, management consulting and other service related firms, manufacturing, oil and gas, pharmaceutical, public relations, retail, transportation, telecommunications, and utilities.

Index

401(k) plan (see Benefits)
409(p) testing 105
Accountants 65
Acquisitions 28, 39, 57, 64, 67
Administration
  (see ESOP administration committee
  or Plan administrator)
Allocation 10-11, 39, 43, 62
Amendments 17, 43
Announcing the ESOP
  (see Rollout meeting)
Annual participant statements
  (see Documents)
Appraiser (see Valuation firm)
Assets 18, 24, 43-44, 55-56,
  79, 81, 84, 90, 92
Attorney 4, 66
Audit 25, 30, 48, 56, 63, 65, 67, 97, 104
Audit Committee (see Committees)
Balance sheet 33, 58, 62, 77, 79-82, 84
Bankers 28, 53, 64, 90-91, 93, 100
Benefits
  401(k) 6, 11, 16, 37-38, 45, 79
  Bonus 6, 30, 97
  Management incentive plan 97
  Phantom stock 30, 97
  Profit sharing 6, 30
  Stock appreciation rights 30, 32
  Synthetic equity compensation 60
Benefit level 36-40, 45, 62-63
Board of directors 4, 11, 23-49, 52,
  56-58, 60-62, 64, 70, 77, 80, 83,
  87-92, 97-99, 101, 104, 105
  Compensation 27
  Independent board members 26-30
  Slate 28-29, 31
Board members
  (see Board of Directors)
Bona fide offer
  (see Sale of an ESOP company)
Bonus plan (see Benefits)
Borrowing base certificate 100
Budget 25, 63, 78-79, 81-82
Business literacy 70-71, 75, 80-82, 85
Buy back shares
  (see Repurchase obligation)
Cash flow 15, 32, 35, 40-41, 62, 79, 81,
  83-84, 100
Certified EO 111
Certified Public Accountant
  (see Accountants)
Chief Executive Officer
  (see Management Team)

Chief Financial Officer
  (see Management Team)
Chief Operating Officer
  (see Management team)
Cliff vesting (see Vesting)
Committees
  Audit committee 30
  Compensation committee 30, 97
  ESOP administration committee 42-45,
  48, 57, 62
  ESOP communications committee 7,
  54, 69-72, 99
  Ethics committee 31
  Executive committee 31
  Nominating committee 31
Communications committee
  (see Committees)
Compensation committee
  (see Committees)
Confidentiality agreements 88
Conflict of interest 27, 59-60
Contingent consideration 93
Continuing education 60
Covenants 53, 100
Covenant testing 100
Culture 4, 26, 37, 53, 69, 71-72, 77,
  85, 91
Deleveraging 33, 65
Department of Labor
  (see U.S. Department of Labor)
Directors and officers liability insurance
  (see Insurance)
Dissolution 56
Distribution 8, 14-17, 31, 38-39, 47, 66,
  93-94, 98, 105
Diversification 13-14, 31, 34, 84, 105
Documents
  Form 5500 18, 48, 65, 102
  Participant statements 18, 43, 45-47,
  49, 65-66, 71
  Plan document 10, 14-15, 17-18,
  42-43, 45, 56, 66-67, 92, 102
  Summary annual report 18, 103
  Summary plan description 5, 17,
  99, 102
  Trust document 5, 18, 55, 61
  Trustee document 61
Due diligence 63-64, 104
Duty of care (see Fiduciary duty)
Duty of loyalty (see Fiduciary duty)
Education programs (see Business
  Literacy or Personal Finance Literacy)
Eligibility to participate 10-11
Employee Financial Wellness Survey 78

Index

Employee-Owned S Corporations of America (ESCA) 60, 70, 72, 111
Employee Ownership Month 72
Equity 3, 32-33, 39-40, 59-60, 62, 65, 79, 80-82, 87
ERISA (Employee Retirement Income Security Act) 44-45, 55, 61, 66, 102
ESCA (see Employee-Owned S Corporations of America)
Escrow 93
ESOP administration committee (see Committees)
ESOP Association, The 60, 78, 99, 111
ESOP communications committee (see Committees)
ESOP fiduciary coverage (see Insurance)
ESOP legal counsel 66-67, 101, 103
Ethics Committee (see Committees)
Executive committee (see Committees)
Fair market value 14, 18, 31, 44, 61-62
Fiduciaries 17, 24, 32, 35, 45, 55, 57, 60, 97, 101
Fiduciary bond 105
Fiduciary duty 23-24, 27, 29, 44, 59-60, 80, 93
Fiduciary firm 57-59, 61
Financial literacy (see Business Literacy or Personal Finance Literacy)
Forecasts 40, 41, 64-65, 104
Form 5500 (see Documents)
Graded vesting (see Vesting)
Great Game of Business, The 82, 111
Gross margin 81
Hardship withdrawal 16
Holdbacks 93
Human Resources Director (see Management Team)
Income statement 77, 79, 81-82
Initial announcement of ESOP (see Rollout meeting)
Insurance 27, 46, 58, 60, 97, 101
   Directors and officers liability insurance 27, 97
   ESOP fiduciary coverage for board members 97
   Key person life insurance 97
Internal loan 62, 104
Internal Revenue Service 48, 59, 61, 65, 94, 101-102
Internal trustee (see also Trustee) 45, 57, 59-61
International employees 11

Key person life insurance (see Insurance)
Legal counsel (see ESOP Legal Counsel)
Liabilities 27, 32-34, 39, 58, 60, 62, 79, 81, 92, 97
Liquidation 56
Literacy (see Business Literacy or Personal Finance Literacy)
Litigation 27, 64, 84
Loan 15, 32-33, 37-38, 53, 62, 79, 104
Loan debt 32-33
Management incentive plan (see Benefits)
Management succession 40-41, 90
Management team 3, 9, 24-26, 32-33, 37, 42, 47, 51-54, 60, 70-71, 76, 80, 83-85, 87-88, 90-91
   Chief Executive Officer 24-26, 30, 51-54, 62, 77, 98-99, 104
   Chief Financial Officer 26, 28, 30, 47-48, 51, 62, 71, 98-100, 102-105
   Chief Operating Officer 26, 51
   Human Resources Director 7, 51, 70, 99, 102-103, 105
Managing to the benefit level (see Benefit level)
Material modifications (see Amendments)
Merger 28, 56
National Center for Employee Ownership 29, 37, 60, 70, 72, 78, 82, 89, 99, 111
National Financial Educators Council 78, 111
Net income 81
Net worth 13, 79, 81-82
Nominating committee (see Committees)
Non-disclosure agreements (see Confidentiality agreements)
Open-book management 82
Operating model 52
Participant rights (see Rights of participants and Eligibility to participate)
Participant statements (see Documents)
Pass-through vote (see Voting rights)
Pay out (see Distribution)
Per-share stock value (see Share price)
Personal Finance Employee Education Fund (PFEEF) 78, 111
Personal finance literacy 75-79, 82
Phantom stock (see Benefits) 30, 97
Plan administrator 4, 18, 25, 34, 42-49, 57, 62-63, 94, 105
Plan document (see Documents)
Profit sharing (see Benefits)
Profitability 8, 75, 77, 81-84
Proposed sale 56, 66, 87-94

Index continued

Public benefit corporations 24
Purchase of assets 92
Purchase offer 87-88, 90, 92
Purchase of stock 92
Qualified domestic relations order 48
Quarterly Meetings 76, 85
Recapitalization 56
Reclassification 56
Recycling shares 36, 39
Redeeming shares 36, 38-39
Regulatory tests 48
Repurchase obligation 25, 31-41, 48, 62-64, 67, 89, 105
  Buy back shares 39
Repurchase obligation study 34-35, 40, 105
Request for proposal 49
Revenue 8, 11, 27, 63, 77, 81-84, 101-102
Rights of participants 17-19
Rollout meeting 4-7, 9, 99
S Election filing 98
Sale of an ESOP company 56, 67, 87-94
  Bona fide offer 88-89
SARs (stock appreciation rights)
  (see Benefits)
Section 1042 (see Tax deferral)
Seller of the company 3-4, 6, 11, 39, 51-52, 59, 90, 98, 100
Selling an ESOP Company
  (see Sale of an ESOP Company)
Share allocation (see Allocation)
Share certificate 98
Share price 12, 15, 35, 37, 39-41, 46-47, 49, 62, 64-66, 77, 81, 84, 89
SPD (see Documents)
Stock allocation (see Allocation)
Stock appreciation rights (SARs)
  (see Benefits)
Stock value (see Share price)
Stress 77-79
Summary annual report
  (see Documents)
Summary plan description
  (see Documents)
Sustainability 25, 31, 36-41, 48, 63
Sustainability study 39-40
Synthetic equity compensation
  (see Benefits)
Tax deferral 11
Tax penalties 16
Taxes 32-33, 82-83
Termination of employment 12, 14, 31, 38, 105
Termination of ESOP 45, 67, 93-94

Termination of Trustee 61
Third-party administrator
  (see Plan administrator)
TPA (see Plan administrator)
Trust 5, 12, 24, 36, 55-56, 61
Trust company 57-59, 61
Trust document (see Documents)
Trustee 4, 6, 18, 23, 25-29, 31, 35, 38, 40, 43-47, 55-67, 88-89, 91-94, 97-98, 101, 104
Trustee document (see Documents)
U.S. Department of Labor 7, 59-60, 67, 77, 101
Valuation 35, 40, 46, 56, 58, 60-66, 84, 88, 97, 104
Valuation firm 4, 28, 35-36, 39-41, 44, 57, 61, 63-66, 97-98, 104
Valuation report 44, 62, 65, 104
Valuation timeline 64-65
Value drivers 47, 52-53, 64, 66, 71, 75-77, 82-85
Value trajectory 35, 41, 64, 66
Vesting 5, 12-13, 17, 45, 48
  Cliff vesting 12-13
  Graded vesting 13
Voting rights 17-18, 56